Business Presentations and Public Speaking

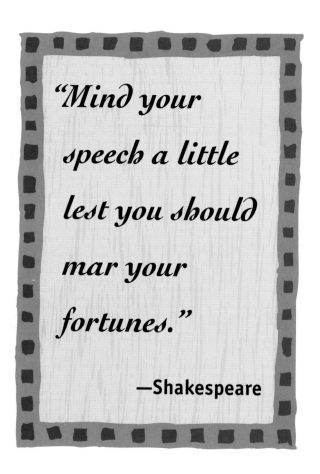

"Mind your speech a little lest you should mar your fortunes."

—Shakespeare

Business Presentations and Public Speaking

CASE IN POINT

RED ALERT!

WORDS TO LIVE BY

McGraw-Hill

New York   San Francisco   Washington, D.C.   Auckland   Bogotá
Caracas   Lisbon   London   Madrid   Mexico City   Milan
Montreal   New Delhi   San Juan   Singapore   Sydney   Tokyo   Toronto

Other *First Books for Business* include:

Budgeting and Finance

Negotiating

Sales and Marketing

Supervising and Managing People

This book is printed on acid-free paper.

Library of Congress Cataloging-in-Publication Data

Engel, Peter H., 1935–
    Business presentations & public speaking / Peter H. Engel.
        p.   cm.—(First books for business)
    Includes index.
    ISBN 0-07-001565-1
    1. Business presentations. 2. Public speaking. I. Title.
  II. Series.
  HF5718.22.E53 1996
    808.5'1—dc20   96-7829
                                        CIP

1 2 3 4 5 6 7 8 9 0 DOW/DOW 9 0 1 0 9 8 7 6

ISBN 0-07-001565-1

Developed for McGraw-Hill by Affinity Communications Corp., 144 N. Robertson Blvd., Suite 103, Los Angeles, CA 90048

Conceptual Development by Mari Florence Editorial and Frank Loose Design

Designer: Frank Loose Design
Developmental Editor: Mari Florence
Production Editor: Nancy McKinley
Technical Consultant: Robert Moskowitz

Table of Contents

Chapter 4: Writing Factors

Chapter 5: Visuals

Chapter 6: Preparation

Chapter 7: Special Factors

Chapter 8: Delivery

Chapter 9: After the Presentation

Appendix

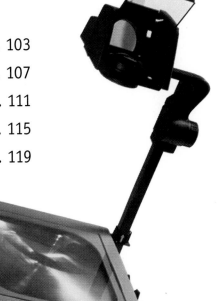

How to Use This Book

We created *First Books for Business* to provide answers to your most pressing questions. In developing this series, we brought together an expert panel of top-notch businesspeople who shared with us their flair for success.

By taking the best of this wealth of information and presenting it in 50 colorful two-page chapters, you'll be able to easily understand the most important elements of the art of doing business. Each chapter features special information elements where you can find help to gain a deeper understanding of the discussed topic. Here's how to best use this book:

1 *Inside Info*
Check out this feature to go behind the scenes and learn what the real pros already know!

2 *Words to Live By*
Read these inspirational, witty, or tongue-in-cheek observations that you can use to motivate yourself—or just for fun.

---

64   PREPARATION

Dressing Appropriately

One of the greatest concerns about making a favorable impression while giving an important presentation is what to wear. Naturally, there is no simple answer. But there are guidelines to help you make an appropriate choice. They include:

Colors and styles of clothing are very difficult to discuss without knowing exactly what you'll be wearing for your presentation and where you'll be wearing it. But a few general rules do apply.

Loud, bright colors are less professional than dark grey or blue, and brown is the least preferred color among professionals and executives.

The latest, wildest fashions are generally less acceptable than classic styles that aren't specifically associated with a particular year or season.

1 Dress as nicely as, or nicer than, your audience. Women generally have more options than men, who should focus on conservative suits or, in less formal occasions, sports jackets and slacks. If you can't be sure, be safe by dressing a little more formally than you think is necessary. It's always easier to loosen up your tie or remove your jacket than to add one you didn't bring with you.

2 Stay neat and clean for the pre sentation. Make your last-minu adjustments— tightening you tie, arranging hair, or retou your makeup before you er the presenta room.

3 Avoid wor or cheap- briefcase watches, such acc Men sho their po achieve look.

WORDS TO LIVE BY

"You are only as good as the people you dress."
—Halston

3 *Skill Builders*
Practice—and master—a new skill that will help you better understand and apply the information you've learned in this book.

4 *TimeSaver*
Look here for shortcuts to getting the job done and insider tips on better time management.

Blending in
Pay attention to the clothing of the people around you. In your own organization, observe the wardrobes of your colleagues and those on and above the level to which you report. Select the clothing you'll wear for your presentation to blend in with what those in the audience will probably be wearing.

TimeSaver
Spend an evening going through your closet to find one or two optimal presentation outfits—including shoes, socks or stockings, and accessories—and look at yourself from all angles in a full-length mirror. When you find an outfit or two that look good, make sure they are comfortable by sitting, crossing your legs, and bending over. If the clothes pass these tests, then put these outfits aside. Top fashion editors recommend putting all the clothes on one hanger along with the tie or other accessories, so you'll have your presentation garb selected and ready to go. You'll then be free to consider other priorities on the morning of your presentation.

CASE IN POINT

As a finalist in the bid for a large architectural firm's printing, James Molina had honed his presentation to a fine tool. The night before the big meeting, he practiced in front of the mirror and hung his best suit out for the next day.

The following morning James was in a hurry to get there early and decided not to take the time to wash his hair or shine his shoes. His logic: He had a great presentation and a great suit—what more could he need?

As it turned out, plenty! James altogether overlooked the fact that architects are detailed-oriented souls. When they noticed his scuffed-up shoes and flakes of dandruff on the shoulders of his "great suit," they wondered if James could give their account the detailed attention it needed. In the end, they awarded the account to another printer.

5 *Case in Point*
Learn how to apply this new information in user-friendly case studies that illustrate the topic and show you how it can work for you.

RED ALERT!

Unless it's for a carefully planned effect—like the tuxedos worn by sports announcers at boxing events—overdressing for your presentation can be just as "gauche" as underdressing. It's a good idea to have at least one outfit in your wardrobe that's "multipurpose"—quality material, conservative cut, dark color—to fit in with any of the wide range of clothing selections you may encounter in an unknown audience.

RELATED TOPICS
➤ Likability and Credibility, (pages 66–67)
➤ Favorable Persona, (pages 86–87)

6 *Related Topics*
See other pages to learn more new and challenging ways of doing business.

7 *Red Alert!*
Watch out for this icon! This tells you situations to avoid, things *not* to do, and red flags you should be looking for.

To make sure you don't overlook any major points, make a rough draft of all the points you want to cover and any ancillary issues that may stem out of them. This list will stimulate your thought process and help you craft a better presentation.

The Parameters of Different Presentations

There are as many different types of presentations as there are types of meetings and conversations. In the largest sense, you're making a presentation every time you talk, or share any kind of information, with one or more people.

Fortunately, most presentations are informal, friendly, and heavily rely on two-way communications, so you needn't go to great lengths in preparation and rehearsals.

But you will almost certainly be asked to make some critically important presentations that *do* require preparation and rehearsal. The two general types of presentations that we're concerned about here and the parameters of each are discussed below.

Sales and Persuasive Presentations

During sales and other persuasive presentations, you're trying to convey a specific opinion, conclusion, recommendation, or point of view. In many cases, you're trying to convince your audience to take a specific action— buy a product, sign off on a project, or perhaps even hire you to work in a certain slot in their organization.

The important parameters for these presentations include:

Your level of belief, commitment, and enthusiasm for the "product" you're pitching

Your expertise on the topic of your presentation

"To communicate, put your thoughts in order; give them a purpose; use them to persuade, to instruct, to discover, to seduce."

—William Safire

Informative Presentations

During briefings and other informative presentations, you're less concerned with the conclusions your audience may reach or the actions that follow. Instead, you're simply interested in bringing them up to speed on certain data, trends, facts, issues, or concerns that you—presumably—know in more detail than they do.

The important parameters for these presentations include:

Your expertise on the topic of your presentation

Your understanding of important facts and issues

Parameters important for *both* types of presentations include:

The location where you'll give the presentation

The number of people to receive your presentation at one time

The length of time you'll have available for your presentation

The motivation, enthusiasm, and level of expertise of the audience who will sit in on your presentation

The importance of using visual aids in your presentation, such as demonstration models, slides, or other visual materials

TimeSaver
Successful presentations are like enjoyable stories: They follow a tried-and-true pattern. Save time when developing your presentation by analyzing previous ones that seem to have worked well. Then incorporate these effective elements into your own presentation.

Note: It's not as important to copy actual words and phrases as the sequencing of important ideas, the timing and pacing of the presentation, the use of visual and audio materials, efforts at audience involvement, and other parts of a successful presentation.

RED ALERT!

It's almost impossible to give a convincing sales or persuasive presentation for a product you don't believe in.

The best way to remedy this situation is to talk with people who, in fact, wholeheartedly endorse the merits of the product, and try to understand their enthusiasm and positive feelings.

Practice your presentation using a product you like, noting the body language and voice emphasis you use. Then copy these same skills and mannerisms when you give the real presentation.

A less honest approach is to try a good acting job. If you do attempt to sell a product in which you have no faith, eventually you may damage your self-esteem, your sense of ethics, or both.

RELATED TOPICS

➤ **Achieving Your Presentation Goals, (pages 10–11)**

Inside Info

Selecting the Proper Presentation Tools

The proper "tool" does the best job, and this holds true not only in manual work such as carpentry but also in making presentations. At the simplest level, all you need is your voice and your body to discuss, explain, and dramatize the content of your presentations. As your audiences grow larger and your material becomes more complex, a picture is indeed worth a thousand words.

Here are some basic tools you might need for various presentations:

Folders and Binding

It's fast, easy, and inexpensive to photocopy pages of information and staple or clip them together as hand-outs for your presentation. But you can make a better impression, and create a longer-lasting document, by having the same pages bound together.

Wall Boards or Paper Tablets

Whether you're working with a small group or an audience of several hundred, a large and easily visible writing area can greatly facilitate communication. A chalkboard, a dry-erase board, or a large tablet of paper are all simple yet effective.

Microphones

Ordinarily, you needn't use a microphone when presenting to small groups or in small rooms, unless, of course, your voice is unusually soft. Big rooms and large audiences, however, make a microphone almost imperative. Modern, light-weight microphones using thin cords or wireless technology can leave you entirely free to work the room, wave your arms, and do anything you'd do without one.

Laser Pointers

These battery-powered wands, about the size of a ballpoint pen, shoot a beam of light that stays tightly focused. You can stand wherever you wish and emphasize what you're saying by pointing at places on any visuals you're incorporating into the presentation.

Video/Motion Picture Projectors

Certain information—like vast panoramas, moving objects, live action, or animation—are best presented on film or video. Make sure the film projector is compatible with the film you're trying to show. It's simplest to show video using a VCR and a TV monitor, but if your audience is larger than 20 or 30 people, use multiple monitors or a video projector. Be sure the projector will throw an image large enough for your audience to see.

Overhead and Slide Projectors

These are time-tested devices for displaying visuals to a large audience. Slides tend to be more photographic and have automatic slide-changing mechanisms that you can operate by remote control. Overhead projectors require manual image changes but enable you to write directly on the image as you project it.

Computer Display Projection Panels

Usually used in conjunction with an overhead projector, these panels are indispensable for presenting anything that must be displayed through a computer.

Multimedia Projectors

Multimedia projectors, the latest adaptation of computer technology to large-audience presentations, amplify not only the computer's image but also its sound. They provide a convenient mechanism for showing any computerized multimedia presentation to more than a few people at the same time.

RED ALERT! Too much technology can overpower a presentation. As a general rule, use the least technology that serves your purpose and meets your presentation needs.

TimeSaver
With a little ingenuity, the materials you create for one presentation can be made useful for other presentations. For example, by citing dates rather than using labels such as "last week" or "last year," a set of slides on baseline data can be used over and over again.

SKILL BUILDERS — Using Presentation Tools

Presentation tools are helpful to people who know how to use them but can be potential disasters to those who do not. That's why it's important to consciously develop your skills in using various projectors, their remote controls, and other tools that you elect to use in your presentations. As you increase in skill, using the tools correctly and powerfully becomes a habit, allowing your presentation content and objectives to be foremost in your thoughts.

RELATED TOPICS

➤ Using Low-Tech Visuals in Your Presentation, (pages 44–45)

➤ Using High-Tech Visuals in Your Presentation, (pages 46–47)

Inside Info

During the preparation for your presentation, take a few minutes and consciously pretend you are your own intended audience. Think about what you already know, and what interests you. Question why you are listening to this presentation, and what you hope to get out of it. Evaluate your points and the way you convey them to see how effectively they hit home.

Then modify your presentation any way you can to increase its impact and importance for your intended audience.

WORDS TO LIVE BY

"The secret of being a bore is to tell everything."

—Voltaire

Establishing Your Hidden Objectives

There's no doubt you want your presentation to be successful. But unless you carefully think through the hidden objectives behind your presentation, you may not know exactly what you mean by "success," or how to recognize whether you're on the right path toward achieving it. There are some general objectives for every presentation.

You almost always want:

- to appear smooth and self-assured during your presentation.
- your preparation NOT to overshadow all the other events going on in your life.
- your information to come across clearly to your audience.
- to use only as much time as has been allotted to you.
- to feel confident before, during, and after the presentation.

By following the techniques and information in this book, you'll be able to achieve these fundamental aims quite consistently. But there will almost certainly be one or more additional objectives specific to each presentation you give.

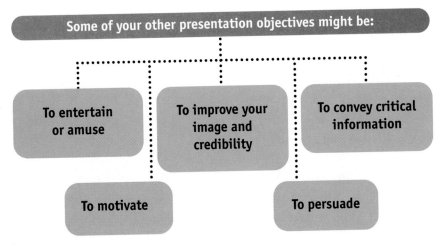

Some of your other presentation objectives might be:

- To entertain or amuse
- To improve your image and credibility
- To convey critical information
- To motivate
- To persuade

You may be able to think of other objectives for your next presentation, but, whatever these may be, remember that the basis of making your presentation a successful one is to know as early as possible precisely what you want to achieve by means of it. Only then can you organize and arrange the presentation to fulfill your objectives.

RED ALERT!

Before you give any presentation, ask yourself two questions: "Why should anyone listen to this presentation?" and "What am I hoping to accomplish by making this presentation?"

If you discover that you're unable to answer both of these questions in simple, direct terms, your presentation probably lacks focus and direction, and you're likely headed for an unproductive experience.

To keep your presentation geared in the right direction, always ask yourself these questions well in advance. Determine the answers, and direct all of your preparation to fulfill these two central purposes.

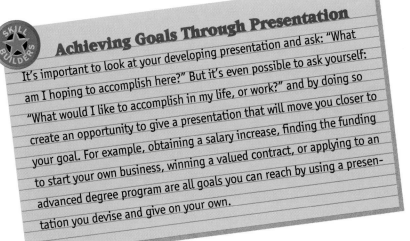

Achieving Goals Through Presentation

It's important to look at your developing presentation and ask: "What am I hoping to accomplish here?" But it's even possible to ask yourself: "What would I like to accomplish in my life, or work?" and by doing so create an opportunity to give a presentation that will move you closer to your goal. For example, obtaining a salary increase, finding the funding to start your own business, winning a valued contract, or applying to an advanced degree program are all goals you can reach by using a presentation you devise and give on your own.

RELATED TOPICS

➤ The Parameters of Different Presentations, (pages 2–3)

➤ Achieving Your Presentation Goals, (pages 10–11)

How Much Time to Take

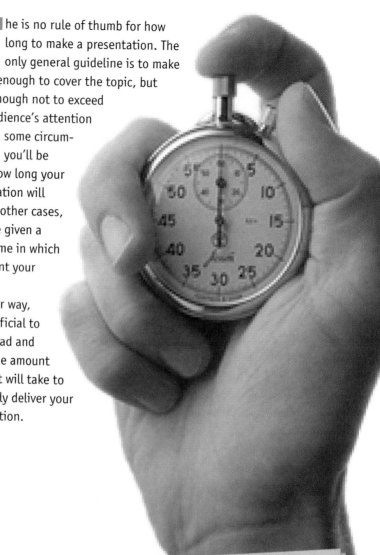

The is no rule of thumb for how long to make a presentation. The only general guideline is to make it long enough to cover the topic, but short enough not to exceed your audience's attention span. In some circumstances, you'll be asked how long your presentation will take; in other cases, you'll be given a time frame in which to present your topic.

Either way, it's beneficial to plan ahead and gauge the amount of time it will take to effectively deliver your presentation.

SKILL BUILDERS

Timing Your Presentation

All audiences enjoy a well-conceived, fast-paced presentation. Practice your talk several times before the presentation date using a stopwatch to time its length. This gives you the luxury of tailoring your presentation to include the information you believe is essential, and it also prevents you from feeling rushed and overlooking vital points you wanted to make.

It's helpful to begin planning your presentation by breaking it down into segments using a timeline like this:

TimeSaver
Organize and index your presentation materials with colored tabs or other quick-reference markings. Then, if you must shorten your presentation or respond to a question in more detail, you can easily jump ahead to the vital information you want to share with your audience.

2 minutes for the introduction

+2 minutes for each main point

+2 minutes for each point under a main point

+2 minutes for each example

+2 minutes for the summary

+2 minutes for responding to each audience question

= TOTAL minutes

Tally up your allotted number of minutes—using this total only as a guideline. Other factors such as the age and interests of the audience, number of people in attendance, time of day, purpose of presentation, and activities planned before, during, and after your presentation should also have a significant impact on how much time you schedule for your presentation.

RELATED TOPICS

➤ Managing Your Audience's Distraction and Concentration, (pages 14–15)
➤ The Value of Rehearsals, (pages 56–57)

One of the best ways to make your presentation more effective is to take notes on previous ones you think worked well. Then add these elements into your own talk. This is particularly true in entertainment, where copying from successful people and giving the material a fresh twist of your own is considered perfectly acceptable.

Achieving Your Presentation Goals

What you want to achieve with your presentation will naturally have a great influence on how you deliver your talk, the elements you include, the presentation tools you select, and much more (right down to your choice of attire and your tone of voice). After you've determined the basic style of your presentation— informative, persuasive, entertaining, or perhaps a combination of these—use the following guidelines to achieve your goals.

For an Informative Presentation

Present a well informed, authoritative image by

- speaking with confidence

- preparing more facts than you deliver so you seem to know a great deal beyond what you're saying

Include facts the audience doesn't already know by

- presenting summaries of new research when appropriate

- giving statistics where they help convey important understanding

- putting the facts in context to help your audience digest your main points

Base any opinions you're offering on these facts by

- building a logical foundation for your conclusions

- showing how other conclusions make less sense

For a Persuasive Presentation

Focus on motivational elements by

- checking and using the audience's desire for positive outcomes (success, higher profits, good project results, etc.)

- playing on the audience's aversion to negative outcomes (failure, lower profits, poor project results, etc.)

Include "guidance points" designed to show you how well you're doing by

- frequently requesting audience consensus on the last thing you've said

- asking your audience to indicate preferences and choices

Motivate the audience to act by

- asking for final agreement with your proposal

- offering "sweeteners" for immediate action

- hinting at problems or losses from delays

For an Entertaining Presentation

Keep the talk moving forward by

- maintaining a brisk pace

- avoiding too much detail

- hinting at what is soon to come

Play on the audience's emotions more than engage their brains by

- weaving in elements of "story" and "myth"

- using music and poetic words

- managing your audience's emotions as well as attention

Continually surprise, delight, and attract attention by

- trying to put a fresh twist on your ideas

- incorporating creative elements wherever possible

RELATED TOPICS

➤ Understanding Your Audience, (pages 12–13)

➤ Drafting the Content, (pages 22–23)

➤ Building Excitement into Your Presentation, (pages 38–39)

Understanding Your Audience

Some simple ways to get to know your audience before you give your presentation include:

- Information get-togethers with some audience members

- Discussions with others who have made presentations to the same group

- Reading the audience members' written histories and biographies

In France, you get your best results speaking French. But in Spain, speaking French won't get you nearly as far as speaking Spanish.

It's the same with presentations. Even though all your audiences may speak perfect English, each one really has its own unique "language" of interests, knowledge, skills, priorities, personalities, and dynamics. If you don't understand the dynamics of audiences, it's very difficult to speak to them in a manner they'll relate to and thus appreciate. Here's what to look for in any audience before you begin a presentation.

Interests

Every group of people has interests—including areas of information they want to absorb and concerns about protecting their existing advantages and benefits. When you know your audiences' interests, you understand how to gain and maintain their attention.

Knowledge

Your presentation on a given topic to a group of beginners will be far different from your presentation to a group of die-hard veterans. It's important to know how familiar your audience is with your subject matter so that you can keep the level of detail and complexity high enough to challenge but low enough to be within their reach.

Skills

Even when an audience lacks specific knowledge, they may have skills, experience, or generalized savvy that improve their ability to follow the information you want to cover in your presentation. By knowing your audiences' skill levels, you have a better grasp of how to make your presentation more successful.

RED ALERT!

Vacant stares, whispered conversations, and/or facial expressions that indicate strong disagreement with what you're trying to communicate—these are early warning signs of an audience you don't understand.

As soon as these behaviors become apparent, *stop* what you're doing. Take stock of what's wrong. Then resume your presentation with a better understanding of your audience. If you don't, you're pretty well guaranteed of wasting your time—and that of your audience.

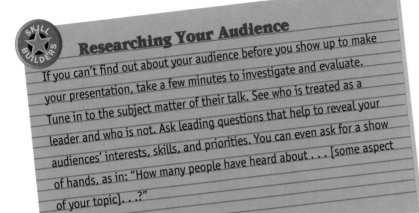

Researching Your Audience

If you can't find out about your audience before you show up to make your presentation, take a few minutes to investigate and evaluate. Tune in to the subject matter of their talk. See who is treated as a leader and who is not. Ask leading questions that help to reveal your audiences' interests, skills, and priorities. You can even ask for a show of hands, as in: "How many people have heard about . . . [some aspect of your topic]. . .?"

Priorities

These are the hot buttons, the motivators, the main reasons your presentation is a welcome one. Find out your audiences' priorities, and you can tweak your presentation to keep them on the edge of their seats.

Dynamics and Culture

Every group has a characteristic pattern of behavior that reflects who is in charge and who is not, who is creative and who is less so, who is respected and who has yet to win respect, and so forth. The members of your audience also work and live within a culture from which they adopt values, attitudes, and behaviors. Although dynamics and culture are often either downplayed or disregarded entirely, they should be studied. Such factors nearly always have a major impact on how well your presentation is received.

Personalities

Some people are receptive to new information and ideas; some are not. Most people have a style and a personality that strongly influence who they respect, listen to, and agree with. By discovering these personality factors within your audience, you can better shape your presentation to gain the highest possible levels of approval and acceptance.

RELATED TOPICS

➤ Increasing Audience Interaction, (pages 20–21)
➤ Likability and Credibility, (pages 66–67)

Every good presentation, even one covering the most important information in the world, contains an element of entertainment. If you don't consider how to maintain your audience's attention, involve their emotions, and provide a solid conclusion, you've wasted a great deal of potential to deliver a terrific and memorable presentation.

Managing Your Audience's Distraction and Concentration

Talking to a class of kindergartners is an exercise in holding people's attention. Although most audiences are more mature than this, there's never an end to the problem of how best to gain and hold an audience's concentrated attention.

If your material and your personality are both highly exciting, you may have little trouble with your audience. But most of us face situations from time to time where we are asked to make a presentation about something that doesn't automatically grab and hold the audience's eye, ear, mind, or heart.

That's why it's useful to understand how to manage both distraction and concentration. Here are some basic techniques:

Have a few attention grabbers

Some speakers grab a nodding audience's attention by pulling out a cap pistol and firing off a few rounds. You needn't go this far, but prepare a few highly sensory experiences that you can whip out during a dull moment. Flags, posters, models, sound tracks, and other "show and tell" devices work well to pick up a drooping level of audience interest.

Utilize pacing

No one but your mother can listen to you for hours on end and be absolutely mesmerized by your brilliance. The rest of us occasionally require some respite.

That's why you should organize your talk into easily digestible segments, units, and modules, each with beginnings, middles, and endings. Demand no more from your audience than an hour of sitting at a time, with no more than fifteen minutes in a row requiring high concentration.

A good way to manage your pacing is to mark up your agenda by segments. For example, you could deliver the first segment of your presentation, offer a brief question-and-answer period, and then break for a few minutes before diving into the next segment.

Provide a brief break

Between your moments requiring deep concentration and total attention, be sure to provide other moments when the audience can relax, regroup, reflect on what you've presented, and prepare for the next moment of depth and complexity.

A five- or ten-minute break is the easiest mechanism to provide this. In addition, you can also pass around pre-printed handouts, delve into background material, or set the stage for your next point.

By doing so, you not only allow your audience time to stretch their legs and relax, but this break time also gives your audience time to further digest what they have just heard.

RED ALERT! Resist the temptation to control your audience by manipulating the conference setting. If the presentation has no diversions, such as relaxing breaks (or, if it is a multiday conference, something to do outside of the setting), your audience will begin to feel "trapped," and will tune out all you're trying to impart through your presentation.

RELATED TOPICS

➤ **How Much Time to Take,** (pages 8–9)

➤ **Building Excitement into Your Presentation,** (pages 38–39)

Overcoming Audience Resistance

It's more crucial when you're making what you hope will be a persuasive presentation, but in every speech, slide show, or chalk talk there's nearly always some need to overcome audience resistance.

Audience resistance stems from the human tendency to retain the beliefs, understandings, and patterns we already know and to reject any information, arguments, or evidence that would logically force us to do something different. Most people also have a strong aversion to making decisions—particularly ones involving money—without taking enough time to get comfortable with the new way of doing things.

Don't let anyone see that their resistance to your presentation bothers you. The more your audience recognizes your vulnerability, the more they'll try to get your goat.

Instead, remain as calm as you can. Find out why the audience appears resistant, and then do what you can to overcome their objections. If they refuse to budge, move on to the next item on your agenda.

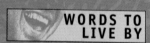

WORDS TO LIVE BY

"You can please some of the people all of the time, and all of the people some of the time. But you can't please all of the people all of the time."

—Abraham Lincoln

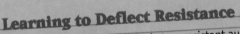

Learning to Deflect Resistance

It's human nature to respond negatively to a resistant audience. By practicing the following steps, you may be able to more confidently address any feelings of insecurity or defensiveness:

- Find an audience member who appears open to your presentation. Focus in on this individual as though you were speaking directly to him or her.
- Put yourself in the place of the audience members. Would you be resistant to this presentation? Why?
- Above all, remember that it's not personal.

STEPS AGAINST RESISTANCE

Prepare Thoroughly

Anticipate the questions and confrontations your presentation might receive from doubters, skeptics, resisters, and even perhaps enemies of your ideas. Prepare your responses so you won't easily be taken by surprise.

Discover the Source

Your first response to any form of resistance should be along the lines of asking: "Why do you say that?" or "Why do you feel that way?" Press the resisters to be specific about their reasons, their understanding of the facts, and their preferences if what you're presenting is, according to them, "no good."

Correct Misapprehensions

Much audience resistance begins when people feel that accepting what you propose will lead to other problems. Sometimes, they're dead wrong about this. If so, it's relatively easy to counter-attack their resistance by getting them to understand what the real facts and relationships are.

Make Adjustments

A large part of audience resistance is based on individuals' unwillingness to accept anything new or different, or to make a change. But this unwilling-ness is often subject to negotiation. If the ideas you're presenting are flex-ible, you can often make enough adjustments to overcome your audience's initial resistance.

Accept Disagreement

Face it. Very few ideas are good enough to be acceptable to everyone. Inevitably, you're going to encounter people who dis-agree with your viewpoints and whose resistance you simply can't overcome. Don't be a perfectionist. Just con-centrate on winning approval for your projects, or on con-vincing the majority, or even just on knowing you did your very best.

RED ALERT!

If you begin to find your-self reacting defensive-ly, take a deep breath and emotionally regroup. When an audience senses anger or hostility from a speaker, it reacts in kind. Avoid this at all costs by being aware of this very natural human tendency.

RELATED TOPICS

➤ Creating a Logical Flow, (pages 30–31)
➤ Gauging the Language Style to Your Specific Audience, (pages 34–35)

Inside Info.

One simple way to handle the person who attempts to dominate by asking too many questions is to move to the other side of the room, where it's harder to see him or her and easier to call on others in the audience.

Taking Questions from the Audience

Nearly every good presentation elicits at least a few questions from the audience. Much depends on the culture. In some community organizations, for example, a ten-minute presentation leads to thirty minutes of questions. But in other business meetings, an hour-long presentation on a controversial issue may generate only one or two polite and superficial inquiries!

How you handle the questioners, and their questions, depends on many factors:

If you want lots of questions:

- At the very beginning of your presentation, offer to take questions whenever they come up.

- Offer encouragement to questioners throughout your presentation, even to the point of saying something like:
  "I can't believe no one has a question on . . . !"

- Keep walking and shifting your stance so you're not looking at—and thereby favoring—just one section of the audience. By doing so, you create a participatory atmosphere where all audience members will feel more comfortable and less inhibited to ask questions.

- Include a brief period after you finish your talk but before you begin taking questions. It's often good to start the transition by asking a question of your own. After a few minutes of reflection, the audience will probably have plenty of questions to ask you.

- Praise the questions people ask you.

If you don't want lots of questions:

- Request that audience members hold their questions until the end of your presentation. This will eliminate at least half the questions you would otherwise be asked.

- Don't praise the questions people ask you.

In addition, sales and persuasive presentations work better when you encourage questions and get your audience involved in a dialogue with you. Briefings and informative presentations are theoretically best when you cover the ground so thoroughly you leave no questions remaining when you're finished. But this is difficult to achieve, and doing so may ultimately be less time-efficient than covering the high spots and actively asking for questions.

RED ALERT!

Be wary of calling on the people who are seated directly in front of you. First of all, they're more obvious to you, so you may be favoring them over people in other parts of the audience. Second, they may have relatively little to contribute. People who sit up front are usually considered to be the most interested, but this isn't always their motive. Often they only ask simplistic questions just to make themselves noticed as participants.

The back rows of the audience are often filled with the least interested people, but they are also the haunts of people most skeptical about what you're saying. If you want challenging questions, look to these rows for inquiries.

SKILL BUILDERS
Responding to Your Audience

Be sure to find some way to begin your response to a question by saying: "That's a good question" or "That's an interesting point." You don't need to be obsequious, or to flatter everyone in the audience, but giving such positive feedback to questioners will tend to elicit more questions.

Never intentionally insult or belittle an audience member. Because you're the presenter, you're in a position of authority. The more you attack a person, the more the audience will side with him or her as "the underdog."

"That's an interesting point."

"That's a good question."

RELATED TOPICS

➤ **Thinking on Your Feet,** (pages 62–63)

➤ **Managing Stress, Anxiety, and Fear,** (pages 76–77)

A tactic used by many smart presenters is to speak to the heart and minds of the audience. Simply translated: Use their language. If you're speaking to engineers, for example, intersperse your talk with topics that are of immediate interest to them. If you're speaking to recording-industry execs, you might tie in some contemporary slang that may be appealing to the audience and could bridge that awkward gap between presenter and audience.

Increasing Audience Interaction

"Please speak up if you have any questions or comments."

If you find your audience a bit glassy-eyed or restive, you can generally improve their reaction to your presentation by special tactics that make them a larger part of the presentation experience.

There are at least five good ways to increase audience participation. Begin practicing them and then use them often.

Ask Questions

"Does anyone have an opinion as to why our outcome for last quarter was so poor?"

The simplest way to get your audiences more involved in your presentations is to ask questions. This is the same technique your tenth-grade history teacher may have used. Why is it so popular? Because it works!

To begin asking more questions, simply work more of your declarative sentences into what? Questions. That's right. How many questions should you ask? Making every sentence a question is boring and obnoxious. But you can ask questions at least how often? Yes, every two or three minutes.

Work Toward Audience Input

 **WORDS TO LIVE BY**

"I wish people who have trouble communicating would just shut up."

—Tom Lehrer

A more sophisticated and complex way to build audience participation is to get them involved directly. For example, you can develop a list of items that audience members contribute, or you can focus temporarily on topics chosen or suggested by the audience.

"Let's pause for a moment and consider the point that Mark Jacobsen brought up."

Play Games

Whether it's Simon Says, the Game of Knots (which requires cooperative problem solving), or Twenty Questions, games provide opportunities for audiences to express themselves, expend stored-up energy, form interpersonal bonds, and participate in the presentation process.

"To help us get in the mood for this discussion, I'd like to start with a group activity called . . ."

Make Teams

A more complex set of games is possible when you divide the audience into two or more teams. You can even pair them up and have each pair work with or against each other to accomplish some task, turning each individual in the audience into a "team of one."

"Now I'd like this half of the room to get together and discuss . . ."

Always try to match the level of the game or challenge to the capabilities of your audience. A game that's too easy or a challenge too difficult will turn them off rather than on.

Some effective ways to use teams include having them analyze and report to the group as a whole on specific topics; develop lists of information or ideas; and make their best proposals on how to solve a problem or capitalize on an opportunity.

Offer Challenges

Dare your audience to find a flaw in your analysis. Declare their inability to work out an equation or develop a plan of action. Challenge their skill in analyzing the consequences of a particular choice or decision.

Most people are highly motivated by a challenge and love the opportunity to show you what they can accomplish if given the right opportunity.

"I'm certain that my figures are accurate, and their impact is quite clear. I don't think there is an alternative, but if someone thinks they can handle . . ."

Getting Your Audience Involved

To engage your audience, see if you can develop at least one of the techniques discussed above into every presentation. You'll see that different techniques work better for some audiences than others, and you'll begin to cultivate the natural rhythm that should occur between good presenters and their audiences.

If your presentation is longer than 30 minutes, try integrating one of these interactive techniques every 15 to 20 minutes. You'll notice that audience enthusiasm will rise each time they're asked to participate.

RELATED TOPICS

➤ Choosing the Most Powerful Rhetorical Strategy, (pages 36–37)

➤ Likability and Credibility, (pages 66–67)

Inside Info

Do your writing on index cards or smaller slips of paper. Put each idea, fact, or argument on a separate card or sheet. It then becomes easier to shuffle and rearrange these elements into the best possible order to achieve your presentation goals. Computer software that allows for fast and easy re-arrangements—word processing or database applications—will also be helpful.

Drafting the Content

Although all presentations contain an element of entertainment and human interaction, even the most artistic mime routine requires some content to connect with the audience. And this content is often your primary reason for making the presentation in the first place. That's why it's important to be sure of what you're going to say *before* you say it.

Your degree of preparation will vary with the length and importance of the presentation, as well as with your level of expertise. At one end of the spectrum, you may do little or no preparation and give a presentation entirely "off the cuff." At the other end, you may spend days or weeks researching your presentation topic, preparing notes, handouts, visuals, and finally rehearsing your presentation until you can do it flawlessly every time. Most presentations will fall somewhere between these two extremes.

Considering only content for the moment, here is a method of putting together your thoughts, facts, and arguments that will work for the vast majority of the "midrange" presentations you will ever give:

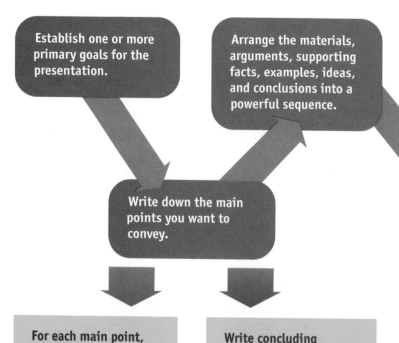

Establish one or more primary goals for the presentation.

Arrange the materials, arguments, supporting facts, examples, ideas, and conclusions into a powerful sequence.

Write down the main points you want to convey.

For each main point, write down the supporting facts, examples, ideas, and arguments you want to give the audience.

Write concluding points: the summary, action steps, or impressions you want the audience to take away with them.

WORDS TO LIVE BY

"... what we prepare for is what we get."
—William Graham Sumner

Backup Materials

Prepare more content than you can use, and keep this extra material thoroughly organized and ready for backup duty. Then, if you're asked to fill more time or your audience asks tough questions, you're better prepared to answer without that sudden "uh-oh" feeling in the pit of your stomach.

"Can you go into more detail regarding your second point?"

Think of smooth transitions between the points you're making. Create a list of them and then insert the transitional statements where they belong.

Rehearse the content to see how it feels.

Practice once or twice in front of a friendly audience who can give you feedback and criticism. Make any final adjustments you deem necessary.

Think of themes that tie all the points together. Put these themes into your introductory remarks.

Go over the pacing in the structure of your content. Make sure to combine balanced moments of intense concentration with lighter moments that give your audience a little relief.

Make any final adjustments you deem necessary.

RELATED TOPICS

➤ How Much Data to Include, (pages 24–25)

➤ Repetition and Content Organization, (pages 26–27)

Inside Info

Your topic will also influence how much content
you can cover in a given
talk. Certain issues, like
tax law or DNA analysis,
take a long time to
explain. Other issues,
like restaurants, the
Olympics, and carpentry,
can be covered fairly
quickly because you
need fewer details to
adequately convey an
idea.

How Much Data to Include

The common question of all presenters is "How much material should I prepare?" Unfortunately, there is no one right answer. The general principle is "Prepare enough to cover the topic without being boring or omitting anything important." The best way to gauge this, however, is through experience.

What's right for your next talk depends on a combination of all the following factors:

Audience Numbers

In general, smaller groups can cover ground faster than larger ones. This means your lecture to one hundred people will probably have to be slower, clearer, and cover less material than your talk on the same topic to ten people the very next day.

Many successful speakers will break down a large audience into smaller groups for further discussion. This allows the presenter to speak "up close and personal" to a larger number of people.

Audience Knowledge

The more expert your audience, the more information you can reasonably expect to cover in a given time period. In other words, your presentations can go into more detail and cover more concepts if you don't have to stop to explain every concept, walk through each logical argument, and show how certain results happen from certain inputs—as you must for an audience that knows very little about the topic.

What to Include

This is a reflection of the old "strategic versus tactical" dilemma that faces every presenter. If you wish, you can abjure all detail and simply deal in basic principles, strategic considerations, and global perspectives. Or you can ditch the generalities and dig into the facts, figures, anecdotes, and "dirty details" of the topic. The more detail you decide to provide in your presentation, the fewer broad topics you can expect to cover.

"Just the facts, Ma'am."

How Much Time

Clearly you can pack more data into a forty-minute presentation than into a ten-minute one. As you gain experience, you'll have a better sense of the relationship between content and time factors. One good way to guess is to extrapolate in a direct line from past presentations: Prepare four times as much material for that forty-minute presentation as you covered in that ten-minute one, for example.

How Fast You Talk

Two people speaking for the same amount of time will comfortably convey very different amounts of information. Again, your best guide to the future is your past performance in similar situations. Carefully reflect on what worked well—and what didn't.

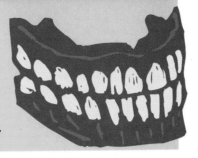

RED ALERT! Try not to feel compelled to fit every last detail into your presentation. It's better to cover a range of topics efficiently than to overwhelm your audience with too much, too fast.

RELATED TOPICS

➤ Selecting the Appropriate Language, (pages 32–33)

➤ Choosing the Most Powerful Rhetorical Strategy, (pages 36–37)

Inside Info

Even if your presentation is full of technical information and details, the main points of your speech should easily fit onto an index card. Use this card to follow an organizational pattern throughout the presentation so that your message is constantly moving forward.

Repetition and Content Organization

The greatest ideas in the world will convince no one of anything if they're poorly presented and—more to the point —weakly organized. The difference between a boring presenting and a top-quality, fascinating one is often simply how the introductory materials, arguments, supporting facts, examples, ideas, arguments, and conclusions are arranged.

1 Introduction and Background

Open your presentation with information that "sets the stage," "sets the mood," or otherwise provides a foundation of data, perspective, and understanding to help your audience understand what follows.

2 Problem Statement

Building on your introduction, it's important to make your audience aware of what problem needs to be solved, what opportunity should be captured, or what issue needs to be addressed. After all, if there isn't such a reason, why are you giving your presentation?

3 Data and Analysis

Here you begin to offer the facts, the information, the stories, the perspective from "on the ground." This part of the presentation content is what your audience your audience nee to make informed choices and decisions regarding the material you covered in your problem statement.

4 Solution Statement

Having brought your audience this far, you now begin to offer a light at the end of the tunnel, a ray of hope, a chance for success. In many presentations, this light, ray, and chance all emanate from the information you're about to offer in the "benefits" part of your talk.

Just as a jigsaw puzzle has one arrangement that lets the picture be clearly seen, so almost every presentation contains material that can be organized in a way to create the most powerful impression on your audience.

In general, make your variations from a proven presentation formula:

RED ALERT!

If the content of your presentation won't seem to fit into a tight, cohesive structure, you may be trying to cram too much information into too short a timeframe, or trying to stretch too few ideas into too many minutes. Try adding or subtracting the points that "don't fit" to see if that improves the structure of your talk. If necessary, fill in more time by providing more detail on points that fit rather than covering extraneous points superficially.

5 Benefits

Now you begin to explain why the idea you're proposing, the plan you're putting forward, or the solution to the original problem statement—regardless of its source—is better than the existing situation. Here's where you bear in mind your audience's interests and priorities.

7 Action Statement

Unless you're briefing people simply for their illumination, most presentations include some form of an action statement, even if it's only a simple message or slogan such as: "Preserve the environment," "Don't spank your children," or "Our company is destined to go places."

6 Summary and Motivational Elements

This portion of your presentation is useful to cement your ideas in place through one more repetition, and to tie your conclusions or action statements to motivational elements—such as "if you want . . ." "to avoid losing what you have . . ." or "there's only a limited amount of time left to . . ."—so that people will be more likely to do what you want.

RELATED TOPICS

➤ **Drafting the Content,** (pages 22–23)

➤ **How Much Data to Include,** (pages 24–25)

➤ **Creating a Logical Flow,** (pages 30–31)

If your presentation is of a timely sort, which would include such things as stock or inventory projections, remember to update this information when revising your presentation.

Revising Your Presentation

Putting together a presentation normally requires more than just throwing together some content. Most often, it demands that you revise and redraft the material to include only the most important elements, to structure those elements in the strongest possible order, and to fine-tune the overall presentation for maximum impact.

Let's take a look at several factors to consider when revising your presentation:

Pacing

Ideally, your presentation will take the precise amount of time you have been allotted. Therefore, aim your revisions to make the presentation the right length, with some additional material in reserve in case things go faster than you planned.

In addition, you should monitor the timing and pacing within those allotted minutes. Keep in mind the following considerations:

• Do you start off and end on strong notes?

• Have you created "high points" within the presentation that are full of energy, excitement, and enthusiasm?

• Will the audience have a chance to recharge and relax between the high points?

   If not, work on providing such a structure as you revise.

Density

Exactly how much is conveyed in your presentation? Is it so dense with information that it requires your audience's full concentration every minute of the time? Is it so light that your audience can follow and grasp your meaning while eating breakfast and reading the newspaper? You want to challenge and inform your audience without overpowering and overtaxing their ability to comprehend your message. Use the revision process to monitor and adjust your presentation's information density accordingly.

Level of Detail

The most important aspect of information density is usually the level of detail. "People aren't turning out to vote" provides information from a strategic perspective. You can back this up with any amount of detail—from a few figures reflecting voter participation in recent national elections to detailed party-by-party and demographic group-by-group voter totals in hundreds of local elections going back several decades. Be aware of the level of detail you're providing, and make sure it's appropriate to your audience, their interests, and what you're trying to achieve.

CASE IN POINT

Bob Mitchell, owner of a new start-up consulting company, was running neck in neck in an electoral race to become vice president of the local chamber of commerce. At his first chamber "mixer," he spoke about crime prevention in the community—a thought on every local businessperson's mind. Weeks before the election, however, the community was up in arms over sewer line repairs, which had torn the roads up, thus preventing customers and clients from frequenting local businesses. As a smart and savvy move, Bob modified his final pre-election speech to discuss alternative parking and access options that could be offered to customers. His quick thinking indicated that he knew the needs of businesspeople and, not surprisingly, he won the chamber election.

SKILL BUILDERS — Presentation Logic

Sometimes the most brilliant thoughts are lost because they're presented in illogical order. To keep the logic of your presentation as compelling as possible, cover each idea just once, and put those ideas in the strongest, most sensible order you can find. Then surround that discussion with necessary introductions, listings of ideas, closing summaries, and concluding remarks to make a complete presentation.

RELATED TOPICS

➤ Creating a Logical Flow, (pages 30–31)

➤ Scaling Down Your Presentation, (pages 48–49)

Inside Info

Some people operate best with the "left" or logical side of their brain, while others operate best with the "right" or creative/emotional side. If you're right-brained, you may perceive logic as less important and more difficult to utilize. But rest assured that others respond very well to it—often better than to your own brand of analysis and motivation to action.

Creating a Logical Flow

Like it or not, people tend to be impressed, persuaded, and motivated by the logical flow of ideas.

The sequence , "We need new equipment. We have a big order coming in. Our present equipment can't handle it effectively,"is far less persuasive and powerful with most people than the sequence, "We have a big order coming in. Our present equipment can't handle it effectively. We need new equipment."

To gain the power of logic for your talks, look to organize your presentation of each idea along these lines:

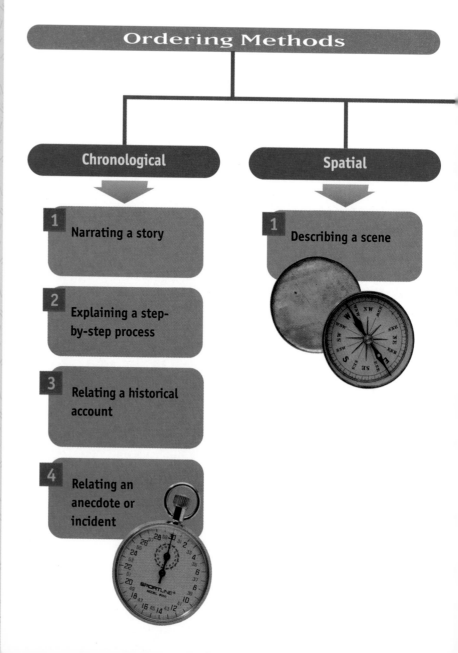

Ordering Methods

Chronological

1. Narrating a story

2. Explaining a step-by-step process

3. Relating a historical account

4. Relating an anecdote or incident

Spatial

1. Describing a scene

Logical Patterns

Chess is a logical game. By making logical moves, a player sets up interlocking defensive and offensive positions in which any one piece plays many roles. In the same way, by making logical arguments surrounding each idea, and arranging those ideas in logical patterns, your presentation becomes an interlocking and thoroughly unified set of ideas that can be highly informative and convincing.

RED ALERT! Logic is not the same as truth. It's simply a well-respected method for thinking. But it, too, has a weakness. If you start your thought process with incorrect assumptions and fundamental facts, you can follow logic quite rigorously and still reach a conclusion that's dead wrong. For example, assume the Moon is made of green cheese, and your logical analysis of what to send in the next Lander will be way off base. So before you put too much effort into your logical thinking, or too much faith in your logical conclusions, be sure to test your underlying assumptions and fundamental facts.

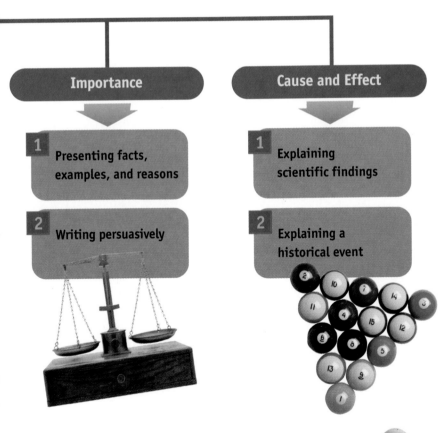

Importance

1 Presenting facts, examples, and reasons

2 Writing persuasively

Cause and Effect

1 Explaining scientific findings

2 Explaining a historical event

RELATED TOPICS

➤ Repetition and Content Organization, (pages 26–27)

➤ Choosing the Most Powerful Rhetorical Strategy, (pages 36–37)

Selecting the Appropriate Language

Your choice of words is a critical factor in determining how well your presentation "goes over" with your audience. If you sound like you're reading from a dictionary, most people will have a hard time following you. On the other hand, if you use the same full sentences again and again to convey certain concepts, your audience will quickly lose interest.

The best language for most presentations is simple, straightforward, and precise without overuse of jargon, slang, or pretension.

Appropriate Language Guidelines

Never use a big word when a small word will do.

Never use many words when a single word will do.

Try to use the same language in your presentation that you would use with a colleague or coworker if you were having a one-on-one conversation on the same topic.

Shorten sentences to less than ten to twelve words. One good way is to allow only one idea in each sentence. Change the leftover subordinate clauses and phrases into sentences that can stand alone.

RED ALERT!

A single word out of place in your presentation can baffle your audience—causing their attention to be distracted while you go blithely on. Result? Your former listeners are left behind and perhaps unable to ever catch up again.

Be very cautious about retaining any unusual, difficult, convoluted, or illogical language in your presentation. Have a very good reason for using it, if you must.

SKILL BUILDERS

Write, Write, Write!

Don't get stuck by language considerations when you're first drafting your presentation's content. In fact, don't think about words at all; just write what you're trying to convey in any words you can find easily. Then, later, allow yourself enough time to go over the presentation and look exclusively at your language. This is when you sit and think about a better word for "rebuttal" or a nicer way to say "we're getting our butts kicked by the competition!"

"I must disagree with my esteemed colleagues, when it comes to the . . ."

"I don't care what those yo-yos think, we should stay the course on this . . ."

Effective Language	Ineffective Language
• Thanks for your input.	• Thank you for taking the time to review my presentation and carefully consider it and offer your responses to each of the items I mentioned.
• We must remain aware of the competition.	• To remain profitable in this ever-changing marketplace, we should always be looking at what our competitors are doing—in terms of products, sales, and vision—and react accordingly.
• To stay competitive, it's important to fully understand today's electronic technologies.	• If we are to remain a force to be reckoned with, all the members of our organization should and must fully comprehend all the aspects of computerization and its implications.

RELATED TOPICS

➤ **Understanding Your Audience, (pages 12–13)**

➤ **Gauging the Language Style to Your Specific Audience, (pages 78–79)**

The best language style to use for 99 percent of your presentations is your own. That is, you'll probably be most accurate, convey the best impression of your own skills and abilities, and allow the maximum amount of your charisma and enthusiasm to come through if you're speaking naturally.

For highly technical or specialized presentations, it's far better to develop enough knowledge to feel comfortable with the necessary language than merely to adopt complex wording in your presentation without knowing much about what it means.

WORDS TO LIVE BY

"Nobody outside of a baby carriage or a judge's chamber believes in an unprejudiced point of view."

—Lillian Hellman

Gauging the Language Style to Your Specific Audience

Because audiences vary from presentation to presentation, it's wise to select a language style appropriate to each specific audience. After all, language is nothing but a tool: You wouldn't want to be caught using a hair curler when what you really need is a kitchen knife. Both are wonderful tools, but they are designed to do different jobs.

That's why you should adjust the language style for each presentation to suit your topic, your audience, and your goals. Consider these adjustments:

Scientific Text
"Many doctors recommend diagnosis by conventional testing such as treadmill or electrocardiogram during chest pain or nuclear valium scans with chemical stress or other techniques, like stress echo, for example."

Professional Text
"The deposition of the defendant could take up to seven days, which translates into a later subpoena date for the remaining five material witnesses."

SCIENTIFIC LANGUAGE

This is the cold, precise language of researchers, doctors, and others who deal in situations and materials most people rarely—if ever—encounter. Because members of the scientific community often deal with unusual matters, they find it more convenient and accurate to employ unusual words. Putting the correct words into your presentation will give it more authority and make it more understandable to such select audiences. But in contrast it will make you seem distant and obscure to average listeners.

PROFESSIONAL LANGUAGE

Similar to scientific language, professional language utilizes highly specific words with precise meanings and connotations. These are useful in conveying a great deal of information in a kind of "shorthand" to an audience familiar with them, but they're equally great at creating distance between you and an audience that's unsure of their meaning.

RED ALERT! Don't try to do an imitation or impression of another person—real or imagined—unless you're very, very good at it. It's too easy to make an unfavorable impression on your audience that will influence how they receive the remainder of your presentation.

TimeSaver

When determining which language style is most appropriate, turn an ear to other presenters who may have gone before you. Ask yourself if they've used a particular style and if it was well received.

Colloquial Text

"The ole boys that you'll be dealing with will treat y'all fairly, provided that you give them enough time to adjust their schedules around hunting season."

Ethnic Text

"After this meeting, let's schlep over to the diner for lunch."

COLLOQUIAL LANGUAGE

This is the everyday language of homes, schools, offices, supermarkets, and the streets. It's also the language most of us know best. Using it in your presentation conveys somewhat the opposite impression from scientific or professional language: demonstrating that you're an ordinary person who has the same everyday experiences as those to whom you're speaking.

ETHNIC LANGUAGE

Similar to colloquial language, ethnic language provides evidence that you're part of a smaller group within the English-speaking community. As a stereotype, it helps your audience quickly identify where you're from, what you've been through, and how you think and feel. While ethnic language brings you closer to certain audience members, it can pull you farther away from others. And, of course, it's often considered poor etiquette to use ethnic language when you don't have the proper credentials, either by birth or experience, to do so.

RELATED TOPICS

➤ Selecting the Appropriate Language, (pages 32–33)

➤ Choosing the Most Powerful Rhetorical Strategy, (pages 36–37)

Choosing the Most Powerful Rhetorical Strategy

Inside Info

Words carry such strong meaning and shouldn't be flung aimlessly about. Consider your words carefully, because strong rhetoric can make the difference when persuading your audience into believing in or supporting your position or product.

Rhetoric is the art or study of using language effectively or persuasively. Originally developed about 2,500 years ago, rhetoric is concerned with using all the elements of language to better achieve the presenter's purpose.

Today we rarely study rhetoric, as those who were educated during medieval and Renaissance times generally did. But because our society so heavily engages in politics, salesmanship, and other forms of purposeful speech, we still have plenty of opportunities to learn about and utilize it.

Rhetorical strategies can be used effectively in the following situations:

In negotiating, rhetoric is one of the tools we can use to persuade those across the table to concede to our requests.

In presentations, rhetoric can be used to create a stronger-than-usual impression on our audience, to increase our credibility and authority, and to marshal the persuasiveness of our arguments.

In argument, rhetoric can be extremely useful in con- vincing others that our facts are more important, our logic is more precise, and our thoughts are more useful than their own.

For example: "While I fully understand what you're asking for, it isn't within my power to agree to this price. Instead, I could guarantee that our existing price will not be increased for a period of time, provided you would be willing to sign a two-year contract to purchase our materials."

For example: "You'll notice on the screen that I've divided our yearly projections into five separate categories. While each category merits its own discussion, you can also see how, interactively, they become one—truly illustrating our company's continued financial growth."

For example: "I'm sure you'll agree that my ideas in this area are stronger and better represent the organization's position on the matter. To begin, the company's long-standing history is not reflected in your report—which I believe is an important selling factor."

Classical rhetoricians such as Aristotle and Quintilian originally established the methods and tools of persuasion and taught that rhetoric could be used in highly specific ways in both written and spoken forms.

RED ALERT!

In many cases, rhetoric can be too powerful for your own good. For example, when drafting a presentation you can become so easily swept up in the power of your own language that you complete an impressive argument but neglect to present facts that back up the data. A presentation that overly relies on rhetorical strategies can also "backfire" when the audience recognizes undelivered promises and prosaic yet meaningless phrases directed toward them.

Some specific ways rhetoric can be used:

The process of rhetorical "invention" involves developing and conveying logical arguments in ways calculated to persuade the audience that your conclusions are correct.

The art of rhetorical "disposition" centers on organizing the various facts, issues, and supporting arguments to most persuasively and convincingly explain one's point of view.

The subject of rhetorical "style" covers various standard techniques for persuading one's audience.

For example: "The basic facts are apparent to all. By permitting this industrial development, the local land values will not only rise substantially but new jobs in the area will more than double over the next eighteen months."

For example: "Change is often a frightening process, which is why I've created this series of charts and graphs to illustrate how beneficial this type of change can be. By reviewing these audiovisual components, I'm sure you'll come to agree that this development will be beneficial for years to come."

For example: "My friends, we all want to find a successful, profitable middle ground. I'm sure that if you thoroughly consider all the elements I've presented today, you'll make the right decision."

SKILL BUILDERS — Figurative Language

The easiest and most popular rhetorical technique is the use of figurative language, which involves "figures of thought"—the arrangement of words to convey a more powerful impact—and "figures of speech"—the manipulation of word meanings to create a stronger impression or convey complex ideas more simply.

RELATED TOPICS

➤ Selecting the Appropriate Language, (pages 32–33)

➤ Gauging the Language Style to Your Specific Audience, (pages 34–35)

Building Excitement into Your Presentation

As we discussed earlier, every good presentation contains an element of entertainment. That means you can use the skills and tricks of the entertainment world to capture and increase your audience's interest level. Building in excitement is one of the best ways to do this.

Let's look at some of the most important elements that contribute to an exciting presentation.

Suspense

Hitchcock movies are masterpieces of suspense. We think we know what's going to happen—because we've seen the bad guy's gun, for example—but before it does, director Alfred Hitchcock makes us wait, and wait, and wait. Then, whether what we expected happens or doesn't, our interest has been held for several minutes.

You can achieve the same effect by lacing your presentation with remarks about "big problems," "easy solutions," "wonderful opportunities," and other interesting things that you'll talk about "in a minute" or "a little later." People will want to know about what you've "previewed" by using these lead-ins, and they'll remain interested in your presentation for longer.

Finding an Appropriate "Capper"

In show-business lingo, a "capper" is something used to take the performance to the next highest level. Obviously, seltzer bottles and whoopee cushions have no place in the business world, so you should look for an element that somehow ties into your presentation.

For example, if you're trying to convince an audience of auto dealers that your floor mats are a great "match" for their cars, consider personalizing books or boxes of matches with your name, logo, and clever slogan. This way, your audience takes home more than just your words.

Thrills

A cap gun going off, a bird flying across the room, a snake popping out of a can, even a sudden declaration of good or bad results—anything you can use to give your audience a little thrill of surprise and shock will help to increase the excitement level of your presentation.

Desire and Fear

The two strongest emotions evoked in most audiences are desire for gain and fear of loss. That's why so much persuasive talk is taken up with pronouncements that this is "the best," "the only," or "the first," and also with notions of "to protect yourself and your family," "limited-time offer," and "first come, first served."

Work elements into your presentation that play on your audience's desire for gain or fear of loss, and you'll immediately gain a stronger grasp on their hearts and minds.

Elation and Triumph

When the good guy wins out over the bad guy, saves the day, and gets the girl, the audience really enjoys the accompanying feelings of elation and triumph. It's the "up" ending that makes the difference between a hit movie and a flop.

You can get the same effect in your presentations if you find a way to portray certain elements of a situation in conflict, and then to resolve that conflict in favor of the good guys. "We've licked cancer!" "We got the contract!" "We beat the deadline!" are just some of the signals that work to create feelings of elation and triumph that your audience will remember and enjoy.

TimeSaver

The saying, "Imitation is the best flattery," has more than a germ of truth behind it. Make a mental note of the methods by which other effective speakers have captured the attention of their audiences, and utilize some of their tools in your own presentations.

RELATED TOPICS

➤ Repetition and Content Organization, (pages 26–27)

➤ Increasing Your Charisma, (pages 68–69)

RED ALERT!

Some formulas are easy to overuse. During the Olympics, for example, you consistently hear that nearly every athlete "got a lot of support from family members" and eventually "overcame adversity" to win a place on the team. Repetition is good, but too much repetition becomes ineffective.

Inside Info

Don't forget that *you* are part of your presentation. Your clothes, accessories, posture, hairstyle, voice, facial expression, and hand gestures all help to convey a world of information about how much you know, how much you can be trusted, and how important your ideas and information might be.

For better presentations cultivate the best personal image and style—from the first word out of your mouth right down to your toes.

WORDS TO LIVE BY

"There is nothing worse than a brilliant image of a fuzzy concept."
—Ansel Adams

Establishing the Image and Style of Your Presentation

Just as you choose the most effective strategies for language and argument, you should also choose the most effective image and style for your presentation.

Here are a few images, or roles, to choose from for different presentations.

The Scientist

Good scientists care only for the observable facts. They base what they say on the results of replicable experimentation. Therefore, to argue or disagree with a scientist is to dispute reality itself.

You can often recognize scientists because they tend to show little emotion—other than excitement at the power and beauty of nature. They throw around a great many numbers, or at least factual statements, and they focus on logic and reason above all else.

The Expert or Professional

Some people erroneously acknowledge anyone with a briefcase as an expert. Cultivating the "image" of an expert or a professional in a given field—with or without credentials—can easily make your presentation a great deal more credible to people whose opinions really count.

In reality, you can legitimately recognize an expert or a professional by his or her depth of knowledge in a particular area. Experts don't always have strong opinions about what is "best," but they do tend to use rather specific language that others may not understand, and they're seldom surprised by any argument or fact, since they've usually already considered it fully in their thinking.

The Consultant or Advisor

This person is primarily interested in finding out what the audience wants to know or do and then deliver it with a minimum amount of fuss.

You can recognize a consultant by his or her stronger emphasis on interpersonal dynamics than on factual matters. For this reason, consultants often spend as much time investigating their audience ("the client") as they do explaining the topic under discussion.

The Interested Party

Having a child gives you instant credibility on matters of schooling, child care, pediatric medicine, social values, gender differences, and other related topics. This proves it's far easier to develop your "bona fides" not by dint of hard work, studying, and advanced degrees, but simply by putting yourself in the position of having the appropriate experiences.

You can recognize the interested party because they tell you right off about their relevant background or experience. "I live in the neighborhood," "I once owned that kind of car," and "I have worked with this bank for years," are all statements that let you know the speaker is an interested party.

RED ALERT! Make sure the image of your presentation is not so completely out of synch with your audience that you become off-putting. For example, an older, conservative group of businesspeople may not relate to an architect with a goatee and sideburns—even if the architect's working style meets their needs perfectly.

Finding Your Presentation's Identity

It's easy enough to spend your whole life becoming an expert or a scientist in one narrow area. But that limits your ability to give convincing and powerful presentations in other areas. That's why it's important to delve into a topic before you give a presentation—at least long enough to gain the kind of image and style you need to achieve your presentation goals.

RELATED TOPICS

➤ Likability and Credibility, (pages 66–67)

➤ Projecting a Favorable Persona, (pages 86–87)

You'll rarely find an audience that leaves a presentation saying: "Everything he said was really dumb, but boy did those slides and overheads look good!" Much more often, you'll overhear remarks like, "Sure, he was drawing on a napkin. But you have to admit he made a lot of sense!"

In other words, it's not usually the quality of your materials that wins over an audience—it's the quality of your thoughts and your message. The materials are merely there to support—or possibly detract from—your thoughts and your message.

Ad Hoc Versus Slick Materials

There was a time when slick presentation materials implied heavy expenses and long hours of preparation time. But today, with computerized "desktop publishing" and "presentation software" that automatically output to professional quality slides, transparencies, and even video tape—as well as to paper—it's almost as quick and easy to have slick materials as it is to have Xeroxed, collated ones. Sometimes, it's even easier.

So the question becomes, Which ones work best for your presentation? Here are some points to remember in making this choice for your next presentation.

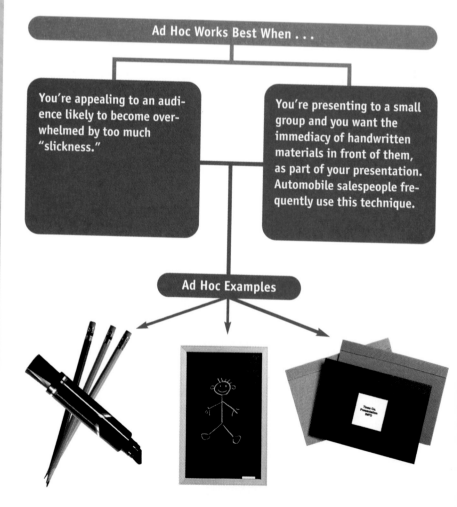

Ad Hoc Works Best When . . .

You're appealing to an audience likely to become overwhelmed by too much "slickness."

You're presenting to a small group and you want the immediacy of handwritten materials in front of them, as part of your presentation. Automobile salespeople frequently use this technique.

Ad Hoc Examples

"It's all in the presentation."

—Julia Child

Creating Presentation Materials

It's easy to get professional-looking materials if you know how to work a good presentation program, like Microsoft PowerPoint or something similar. Just type in the text, and the software creates nice-looking slides or overheads. If you wish, you can tweak the appearance by shifting blocks of text, changing type fonts, or adding some clip-art style of graphic images.

It's even easier to get ad hoc materials. Your local art store has a variety of paper and markers, "press on" or "rub on" lettering, and more.

RED ALERT!

Regard-less of your choice of ad hoc or slick materials, don't confuse the *appearance* of your materials with their content. Even the worst-lettered handmade sign should have a strong, cogent message that furthers the purposes for which you are making this presentation.

Slick Works Best When . . .

You have complex relation-ships to convey, and the wrong location or size of a single element within your materials can easily convey the wrong meaning. Maps, for example, are difficult to make accurately by hand without several attempts.

You're presenting to a sophisticated audience and have been given a great deal of time to prepare. They're so accustomed to slick mate-rials that showing them pen-cil drawings on scraps of paper will interfere with their hearing what you have to say.

Slick Examples

RELATED TOPICS

➤ **Using Low-Tech Visuals in Your Presentation,** (pages 44–45)

➤ **Using High-Tech Visuals in Your Presentation,** (pages 46–47)

Using Low-Tech Visuals in Your Presentation

The lowest-tech visual aid is probably a chalkboard. It's on a continuum of technology that includes many familiar items—from several different forms of marker boards, large paper tablets, or charts all the way up to the large reflective screens that display slides and overhead transparencies.

We've been seeing these items since elementary school, so most of us assume we know how to use them effectively. Wrong! Most of continually make the most basic mistakes in using this "low-tech" equipment for our presentations.

Whether you're using a chalkboard, an overhead projector, or anything in between, consider these factors carefully:

Placement

Sometimes you don't have the opportunity to set up the room for your presentation, so you feel stuck with what the audiovisual technician has done—particularly when everything is taped carefully into place. But it's worthwhile to see if it's feasible to move things around so that:

- You're at the center of the "stage" area at the front of the room.
- Your podium or note stand is slightly to your left (if you are right-handed people).
- Your chalkboard or projector screen is a few feet to your right (place both of these the opposite way if you are left-handed).

This arrangement places you—and your presentation—at the center of the audience's attention and physically relegates your visual material and your lecture notes to their true role of supporting material.

Changing the Visuals

As smooth and automatic as most slide and other projectors can be, it's nearly always better for you to pause when you change visuals. Why? Because the change prompts your audience to look at the new material. They could easily miss what you say next. Why compete with your own material?

Instead, initiate the change of visual material—whether you're turning a page or showing a new slide—and simultaneously pause in your presentation. Take a full breath. Look at the new material for a few seconds, then look back at your audience and begin with your new thought.

Frequency

Unless you're presenting lots of photographs or other audiovisual material, it's best to limit the changes to no more than once every 60 to 90 seconds. More often than this, and you're dizzying the audience to the point where they'll miss the content of what you're saying.

Pointing

With the arrangement of your supporting materials so that you're the center of attention, don't lose this advantageous position by turning away from your audience. Keep your body facing the audience as much as possible. If you want to point to something on one of your visual aids, use a laser pointer or a big stick.

If you must use your index finger, use the one closest to the screen, so that you can continue facing the audience while you point and speak.

TimeSaver
Once you find a natural "flow" of integrating low-tech visuals, you'll find the tools will naturally integrate themselves into your presentation and you'll become more comfortable using them.

RELATED TOPICS

➤ Ad Hoc Versus Slick Materials, (pages 42–43)

➤ Simple Rules for Better Visuals, (pages 52–53)

Using High-Tech Visuals in Your Presentation

O nce you get past the simple, traditional presentation tools you've known all your life, you move into a new spectrum of advanced technology that has impressive power to improve the captivating, informative, persuasive, and entertainment aspects of your presentations. Largely harnessed to computer power, these presentation tools include a wide array of equipment that can do everything from simplify and speed the preparation of slides, to convert numerical and other data automatically into both static and dynamic graphics.

In other words, you can enter some numbers and formulas into a computer, and have it almost immediately display a bar chart, pie chart, line graph, or other visual display of that information. Then you can change those numbers—say, through some kind of "what if" scenario or series of scenarios—and in real time create new charts showing the current information in place of the old.

In addition to displays of numerical data, the computer also makes it easier to display text and to modify and update it for greater audience interest and more accurate presentations. Once you get the information into a computer—which you can do relatively easily by scanning or electronic transmission—you can then display the numbers, graphics, or other visual elements to small audiences of as many as half a dozen or so right on the computer's own display screen.

As your audiences get larger, you can use see-through projection panels or high-power display projectors to put the computerized information on larger screens. You can also use computer power to create slides and overhead transparencies far cheaper, easier, and faster than you can without the computer. Literally, whatever you produce on the

Revising Old Visuals for New Presentations

Let your presentations and your creative skills build on each other. Save past computerized presentations, for example, and start a new one—not with a blank computer screen but with your most recent opus. You'll find that changing the words, adjusting the visuals, and adding one or two new elements or special effects is much faster than starting from scratch.

computer screen can be printed on the transparent film and put into your presentation's audio package.

Some software also allows for degrees of animated visuals. Words, numbers, and pictures can change color, become highlighted or underlined, physically move across the screen, and transform (or "morph") into other images.
So-called multimedia capabilities are now making it fairly easy and fast to tie
a wide variety of sound, pictures, animation, and film or video into a single
computerized presentation.

RED ALERT! Murphy's Law—that anything that can go wrong
will go wrong—
applies to high technology
presentations with a ven-
geance. Be prepared with
appropriate backups—data
disks, computers, display
systems, power supplies,
cables, and so forth—as
much as possible.

High-Tech Presentation Guidelines

1 Keep presentations practical. Some of the technology
is still fairly new—and thus
somewhat unpredictable.
Don't get bound into a presentation you can't give on
a reliable basis when and
where you need to. If a certain piece of presentation
technology is at all questionable, select a more reliable method of getting your
point across.

2 Don't let the medium overwhelm the message.
It's very easy to become so enamored of these
new tools that you use them too much and allow
the audience to be swept away in an experience
that does little to convey your meaning or accomplish your purposes.

RELATED TOPICS

➤ Ad Hoc Versus
Slick Materials,
(pages 42–43)

➤ Adding Impact to
Your Presentation,
(pages 50–51)

Inside Info

Writing tight, powerful presentations requires patience and skill. Always consider the following:

- Budget time for a final "tightening" pass through your presentation

- First look for any words or phrases you can remove without changing the meaning

- Then look for shorter ways to say what you've said at length

Scaling Down Your Presentation

If you're interested in making a good presentation, you'll almost certainly overprepare. That is, you'll do more than enough research, gather more than enough material, prepare more than enough visuals, and plan more than enough to say. Remember, though, that in presentations as in life, "less" can often be "more."

That's why you must stop yourself from overwhelming your audience and learn, instead, to scale things down to manageable proportions without sacrificing the power of your presentation. Here are some basic ideas for keeping your presentation short, sweet, and strong.

WORDS TO LIVE BY

"Excuse me for writing such a long letter. I didn't have time to write a shorter one."

—Anonymous

1 Don't overwhelm with facts.

Give a few representative ones, instead. For example, on the aging of America, it may be enough to point out that the fastest-growing segment of the population is those over age 75. And the second fastest—those over 85.

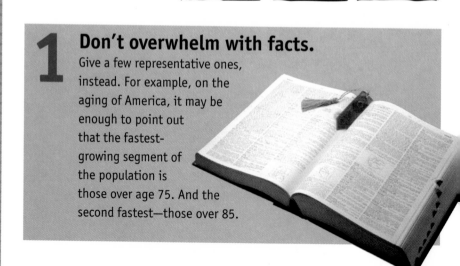

Don't take too long.

Leave your audience craving more information from you, rather than less. A good rule of thumb is to cut from the presentation five minutes more than you'd really like to. If necessary, you can always use the extra details you deleted to fill more time or to answer any questions from the audience.

Choose the perfect method.

Concentrate on finding images, concepts, parallel situations, and other meaning-rich methods for cramming more ideas and information into fewer words, pictures, and seconds of elapsed time. This takes work, but it's well worth it. For example, instead of talking about educational problems, in general and straightforward terms convey the image of high school graduates who are unable to read their own diplomas!

TimeSaver

The quickest way to scale down your presentation is to refer back to your original outline. What were the main points you wanted to make? Based on this evaluation, you can cut out much of the excess information from your speech.

Opening Presentation Tips

It's never easy to scale down material into a shorter, tighter presentation. One of the best ways, however, is to eliminate some of your opening material. Inexperienced presenters often spend the first few minutes of a presentation wasting time by "warming up" to their topic.

Try eliminating everything in front of your first main point. Then replace it with a sentence, or paragraph, that moves your audience into the topic. A good example of a complete introduction: "Sled dogs are likely to become a lot more important in your life than you ever expected."

RELATED TOPICS

➤ How Much Time to Take, (pages 8–9)

➤ How Much Data to Include, (pages 24–25)

Adding Impact to Your Presentation

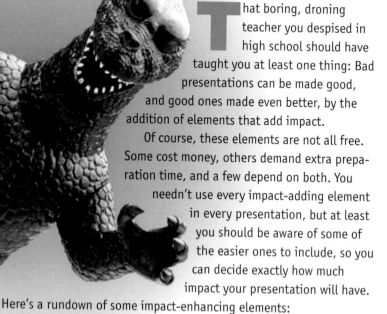

That boring, droning teacher you despised in high school should have taught you at least one thing: Bad presentations can be made good, and good ones made even better, by the addition of elements that add impact.

Of course, these elements are not all free. Some cost money, others demand extra preparation time, and a few depend on both. You needn't use every impact-adding element in every presentation, but at least you should be aware of some of the easier ones to include, so you can decide exactly how much impact your presentation will have.

Here's a rundown of some impact-enhancing elements:

Sound

Just for fun, watch an action movie on TV with the sound turned down. You'll discover that sound creates at least half the impact of the overall presentation.

If you have a high budget for your presentation—a rollout of a new product, for example—consider adding live or prerecorded music that emphasizes the emotional highs and lows for the audience.

But even on a low- or no-budget presentation, you can add some music or sound effects to "punch up" the impact level.

Motion

Singers move when they perform. Movie, stage, and TV shows go to great lengths to include movement and action. Why should your presentation make do with any less?

Gestures, body movement, and even motion of objects around the stage or room all help to focus your audience's attention, convey information, and increase the impact of your presentation.

Color

Green conveys warmth and comfort; blue authority and power; red excitement and energy; yellow warning and danger. Consider this and other factors in consciously deciding on the color of your attire, your presentation materials, your handouts, and everything else in your audience's view as you give your presentation.

Light

The total amount of light that shines on you is a big factor in determining how much attention you'll receive from your audience. If you're no better lit than your surroundings, you'll fade in importance. If the room is somewhat darkened but you're well lit, you'll likely have more impact.

Changing the lighting *during* the presentation can further increase the impact level. While not practical in every situation, spotlights, colored background lights, and moving lights to catch and hold the audience's attention may offer ways to maximize your impact on the audience.

RED ALERT!

Every audience has expectations. Slightly surprising them will increase the impact of your presentation, but going too far will turn them off and reduce your overall impact. So use your judgment in gauging the degree of extra "punch" needed to keep your audience with you.

For example, presenting a new product with a prerecorded trumpet fanfare may add impact. But having a team of twenty Elvis impersonators skydive onto the stage carrying the new product may be overkill that reduces the final impact of your presentation.

Increasing Presentation Impact

Creating a high impact presentation is not very difficult, but it does require that you pay attention to the degree of impact you're likely to have and the steps you need to take to increase it.

For example, in presenting a new product, you can leave it in plain view while you introduce it. Or you can have it revealed at the proper moment by suddenly opening curtains. Or you can open the curtains and set off smoke bombs. Or you can add dramatic music to further add impact to the curtains and smoke. And so forth.

RELATED TOPICS

➤ **Managing Your Audiences Distraction and Concentration,** (pages 14–15)

➤ **Building Excitement into Your Presentation,** (pages 38–39)

Simple Rules for Better Visuals

With today's powerful graphic tools, it's relatively simple to create a pack of slides or overhead transparencies for a presentation. But the mere act of having a visual doesn't mean it's an effective one! We sometimes forget that our sophisticated technology can just as easily create a bad-looking, confusing slide as it can an aesthetically pleasing, instructive one. The trick is to be able to distinguish one from the other—*before* your audience lets you know you've done them wrong.

Visual Guidelines

No more than four or five bulleted points per page. If you include more, you're probably confusing rather than informing your audience.

No more than two lines of text per bullet. It's a visual aid, not a reading test. If long statements are so important, put them into a package of handouts.

No more than one or two graphic elements—pictures—per page. Look at newspaper and magazine cartoons. They convey a single idea—powerfully! Unless you know your visual is doing the same, eliminate it.

If a person in the back row with normal corrected eyesight can't easily and comfortably read the words you're showing, then the typeface is too small.

Type Guidelines

Use no more than two different type faces on a single visual, and no more than five different typefaces through a single presentation. It's OK to use different typeface sizes.

Keep the type fonts simple. Type faces without those little "serifs" are best for larger headlines, while faces with the serifs are best for reading large blocks of material.

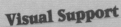

Visual Support

Think of the visuals as the pillars of a suspension bridge: They should carry the main weight of what you're saying but leave plenty of room for you to speak knowledgeably about important matters before you put up the next one. Ask yourself if one or more of the following visuals would enhance your presentation:

- graphs
- diagrams
- charts
- tables
- photos/illustrations
- symbols/equations

RED ALERT! Even if you think it fits that doesn't mean it belongs. It's easy to cram that extra word, those extra thoughts, or that extra bullet onto a page, slide or transparency. Resist the notion. Instead, make sure that all the points you've already listed are really necessary, and further check that you've stated every one in the fewest, simplest words.

Visuals fall into six basic categories: graphic and statistical diagrams, graphic organizers, charts and tables, time displays, process diagrams, an representational diagrams.

Visual Categories

Graphic/Statistical

Picture graphs
Bar graphs
Pie charts
Line graphs

Graphic Organizers

Hierarchical diagrams
Relational diagrams

Charts & Tables

Check list
Mileage charts

	a	b	c
1			
2			
3			

Time Displays

Clocks
Calendars
Time lines
Seasonal Charts

1746 —|—|—|—→ 1946

Process Diagram

Sequential diagrams

Representational

Photos
Illustrations
Symbols
Maps

RELATED TOPICS

➤ **Ad Hoc Versus Slick Materials (pages 42–43)**

Using Handouts Effectively

When handouts were relatively difficult and time consuming to produce, many presenters simply didn't bother with them. But now that so many people prepare their presentations on a computer, where you can press a single button and watch beautiful handouts roll out of the printer, they're far *too* common—and in fact can be counterproductive.

Before preparing handouts to accompany your next presentation, ask yourself the following questions:

Do I have additional, relevant material that my audience should take home with them?

Do I have additional, relevant material that makes more sense to be distributed rather than jotted down by the audience?

Do I have additional, relevant material that I can't cover directly and fully in the body of my presentation?

Only if you answer "yes" to all three of these questions should you go on to prepare accompanying handouts.

Assuming you've decided that handouts are truly necessary, make sure you don't allow them to destroy or de-emphasize the importance and impact of your presentation.

If you pass out materials before or during your talk, people will read instead of listen. It makes more sense to announce that handouts will be available, particularly during passages dense with facts when your rapt audience is scribbling furiously. But withhold the paperwork until you've finished everything but taking questions from the audience.

If you've done the presentation correctly, each of your visuals carries important material and conveys it powerfully and succinctly. It makes perfect sense for you to include them in your handouts. Most presentation software allows for very simple reproduction of your visuals, even "ganging" them several to a printed page.

Supplement the visuals with additional words and pictures, if necessary, to aid your audience members in visually recollecting your presentation a few weeks, months, or years later.

TimeSaver
If possible, recycle the elements in your handouts and use them again and again in other presentations.

Protect the power of your presentation by following these simple rules

Reproduce your visuals.

Save your handouts for the end.

Question and Answer—Handout Referral

If you're getting a lot of repetitive or simple questions from the audience and you don't want to take the time to answer them fully, refer the questioners to your handouts. Not only will your audience be appreciative of the take home materials but you'll also save a lot of time during the actual presentation by issuing responses to their questions such as: "That's a very good question. So good, in fact, that I've included the facts you're looking for on page 14 of my handout."

RELATED TOPICS

➤ Taking Questions from the Audience, (pages 18–19)

One thing most people forget to rehearse is making eye contact. It takes a certain amount of practice to keep your mind focused on your material while you shift your eyes from one person to another in all corners of the room. That's why it's wise to rehearse with a view not only toward speaking what you want but doing what you must to give your presentation maximum power.

The Value of Rehearsals

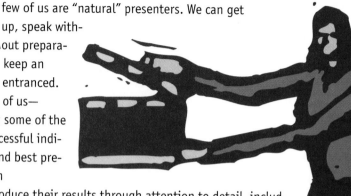

Afew of us are "natural" presenters. We can get up, speak without preparation, and keep an audience entranced. But most of us—including some of the most successful individuals and best presenters in town—produce their results through attention to detail, including the detail of rehearsals.

If you mentally compare several presentations you've attended, you'll note that the best ones were performance-like in their delivery. This is due to the value of rehearsals.

There are at least five elements of your presentation that you should test by going through one or more rehearsals. Each element involved in presentation rehearsal is discussed in detail below.

1 Timing
Can you fill your allotted time slot with important material? Do you need to add or cut? How fast or slow should you go to hit the high spots of your presentation at just the right times?

2 Intonation and Emphasis
It's almost impossible to do a "cold" reading of material with all the right emphasis and intonation—even when you've written it! That's why the best presenters rehearse what they're going to say, With a particular focus on remembering which words in the sentences get the "oomph" to create all the desired impact on their audience.

3 Technology Problems
Go through the motions of changing the slides, pulling down the projector screen, turning off the lights, and turning on the tape player. It's the only way to be sure all those switches switch, light bulbs light, and motors whir as they should.

WORDS TO LIVE BY

"Practice makes perfect."

—Anonymous

4 Confidence Level

A presentation nearly always comes off better when you feel confident about your ability to deliver it. Rehearsals are important because—quite simply—they help boost that confidence level.

5 Test Audience Reactions

Aside from technical and personal considerations, rehearsals provide an unbeatable opportunity to test your presentation on an audience and see how they react. Whether the "mock" audience is your family, friends, colleagues, or strangers, they provide a benchmark that helps you gauge the impact your presentation is likely to have when the chips are down and your reputation is on the line.

RED ALERT!

As mentioned earlier, Murphy's Law operates in most presentation situations. Try not to be overconfident, regardless of how good your reasons and how excellent your track record as a presenter. Use at least one rehearsal to check electrical connections, equipment function, and the sequence and completeness of your material, as well as your understanding of it and ability to deliver it with meaning and emotion.

If you don't rehearse, you're creating an opportunity for what is now a tiny problem to explode into a major disaster during your actual presentation.

CASE IN POINT

Recently, a local politician read the eulogy during the funeral services of a cadre of fire fighters who had died while battling a forest fire gone awry. His profound and comforting words to the mourners came to an abrupt halt when he said the line, "And God looked down on these people and said, 'Well done.'"

The families of the victims were horrified by this speech, which equated their loved ones with char-broiled meat. Although the politician was well intentioned, he obviously hadn't rehearsed his speech and thus ended up offending a great deal of people while also embarrassing himself.

This type of egregious error can be minimized by running the text of your presentation by another person—preferably someone who understands the meaning and context of the speech. Follow this simple rule and you'll be less inclined to be misinterpreted and misunderstood.

RELATED TOPICS

➤ **Building Excitement into Your Presentation,** (pages 38–39)

➤ **Preparing for Interruptions,** (pages 58–59)

Occasionally, an audience member will begin to interrupt because of his or her enthusiasm for your topic. Take this interruption as a compliment, and then assure the person that you will be available to answer questions following the presentation.

Preparing for Interruptions

From comedians to top executive briefers, almost everyone who gives a presentation has to cope with unexpected questions, comments, criticisms, and other interruptions to the smooth flow of ideas you've so carefully planned.

Since you can't avoid them, your best bet is to prepare for them. Here are some guidelines to help you:

1 *Know Your Material*
Because an interruption is like a bump in the smooth highway of your thought and presentation, it's easy to be distracted by it. The best remedy is to be so familiar with your material that virtually no interruption can take you into uncharted territory.

Thorough preparation allows you to listen to a question, comment, or criticism and fit both it and your response into the overall flow of your presentation and how you want to reach your conclusion.

WORDS TO LIVE BY

"It's not polite to interrupt."

—Mom

Unfortunately, some people enjoy interrupting a speaker just to create a fluster or demonstrate their own power. In a sense, an interruption is a test of wills. If you find this unacceptable, you can continue speaking until the interrupter peters out or is shouted down by other members of the audience.

2 *Stick to an Agenda*

Like a map, an agenda (usually in outline form) is a good tool for keeping yourself on course as you make your way from the introduction to the inescapable and compelling conclusion of your presentation.

Depending on circumstances, you may find that you must digress to answer an interrupter's questions, or you must pause to deal with a balky slide projector or an interloper who asks directions to the men's room.

Whatever interruptions may occur, you can more quickly find your place in your preplanned train of though by glancing at your agenda to see where you left off.

3 *Remain in Control*

Since you've been asked to make a presentation, you rightfully belong in control of it. That is, no matter what questions are asked, the order of presentation that *you've* decided on almost certainly makes more sense than any other. So stick with it!

This means you should avoid leaping from topic to topic in response to interruptions from the audience. If the question points to an unimportant topic, you can promise to respond to it in the question-and-answer period after your presentation. If it's an inquiry, you can promise that you'll come back to it in due course, after you've covered some necessary and enlightening preliminaries.

In either case, you'll make a better impression and deliver your message with greater impact when you remain in control of your presentation and carry on to the end, despite any interruptions that may occur.

RELATED TOPICS

➤ The Value of Rehearsals, (pages 56–57)

➤ Four Presentation Phobias and How to Overcome Them, (pages 78–79)

How to Present Bad News

If you have a close relationship with your audience, you may intuitively know the best way to present them with any bad news. If not, try to be quick—but not brutal—about delivering the unpleasant information. Generally, it's best to offer some very brief introductory remarks that let the audience know they should get set for a gut-wrencher. Then deliver it. Give your audience a brief time to absorb what you've told them and then move on to the next order of business.

It's every presenter's nightmare to have to announce, "Sir, your project just died." It doesn't matter whether you're talking about a fondly held idea or a fervently promoted project. Any time you're the one to tell an audience bad news—that is, information they don't want to hear—you're automatically in a difficult position.

But you don't have to take it lying down. You can use several techniques to lessen the audience's negative reaction to your presentation of bad news. These include:

Be Frank and Honest

Some people try to soften the blow of delivering bad news by such strategies as hemming and hawing, working up to it, or hoping the audience will guess what you're trying to say. The net result, though, is just to make the situation—and your audience's reaction to the bad news—worse.

The best way to break bad news is to be sympathetic and honest. Carefully explain the situation—without making excuses—and allow your audience to ask questions. Don't allow yourself to become defensive if an audience member reacts poorly. Maintain your composure throughout, and your audience will respect you for it—even if they don't like what they hear.

Find a Positive Angle

Don't try to sugarcoat the bad news, but do try to tie-in the undesirable information with some positive angle.

If there is a way to remedy the problem, introduce one or two possible solutions to the audience. This opens the floor for dialogue, rather than finger pointing. Two examples would be:

For a business failure   For a negative decision

". . . there will be other, even better opportunities in the future.".

". . . at least we've learned some valuable lessons."

Message versus the Messenger

In Roman times, bringing bad new to the emperor was a shortcut to a death sentence. Today, people retain that same instinctive desire to lash out at the bearer of bad tidings.

That's why it's important to draw the widest possible distinction between yourself and the sources of or reasons behind the bad news.

You'll be insulated from any fallout from the bad news if you can honestly say: "I didn't *cause* that fire. I'm just telling you about it."

Do not, under any circumstances, lose your temper if the situation becomes heated. Realize that your audience is experiencing a natural reaction to bad news and help them understand the situation by being open and available for their questions and criticisms.

Offer Sympathy and Support

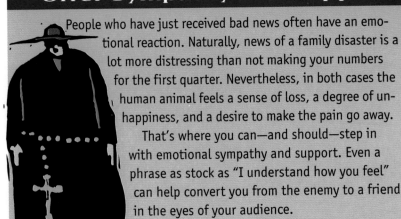

People who have just received bad news often have an emotional reaction. Naturally, news of a family disaster is a lot more distressing than not making your numbers for the first quarter. Nevertheless, in both cases the human animal feels a sense of loss, a degree of unhappiness, and a desire to make the pain go away.

That's where you can—and should—step in with emotional sympathy and support. Even a phrase as stock as "I understand how you feel" can help convert you from the enemy to a friend in the eyes of your audience.

RELATED TOPICS

➤ **Preparing for Interruptions,** (pages 58–59)

➤ **Thinking on Your Feet,** (pages 62–63)

Inside Info

One of the best ways to get out of answering a difficult question is to fill the air with facts. As you prepared for your presentation, you probably learned many hard facts. By weaving them into your answer, you can safely avoid treading into dangerous territory.

Thinking on Your Feet

Read my lips. No new taxes." Whether you're a presidential candidate or an aspiring assistant bookkeeper, it's almost inevitable that you will encounter situations requiring you to think fast and spit out answers that—if wrong—will haunt you for years to come.

Generally, the problem comes up when you're asked a tough question. If you're prepared for it, you can probably give a "canned" answer that won't get you in trouble. But if you're facing an unexpected question, you can easily blurt out the wrong answer—even before you realize the full and possibly disastrous implications of what you're saying.

If you think you may be called on to give presentations in the future, expect that these situations will often come up. That's why it's important to cultivate the ability to think fast and effectively on your feet.

In the meantime, however, you can use some of the following relatively simple techniques to avoid the dreaded "foot in mouth" disease.

Pause.
It's always a good idea to take a moment before shooting off your mouth. This generally makes you seem more intelligent than you feel at the time.

Say:
"That's a good question. Let me think about it for a minute." This approach outrageously flatters the person who asked you the question. It also gives you some time to formulate a response.

Developing Body Language

Body language is critical in tough situations. Verbal toughness looks more like empty bravado when your body language doesn't back up your choice of words.

To make sure it does, concentrate on standing tall; using simple, strong gestures; and maintaining eye contact with your audience, and particularly with the person asking the tough question.

RED ALERT!

In difficult situations, some of your audience may actually want to sandbag your presentation. Aside from trying to harm you and your career, they may have their own reasons for trying to bring down anyone who happens to be in your position.

Be alert to such possibilities, but don't take them personally. Instead, focus on getting out alive. Offer careful answers to dangerous questions and take every opportunity to switch the subject back to your positive presentation track.

Review.
Just because an idea for a response pops into your head is no reason to let it run out of your mouth! Instead, try to perceive your answer from other people's points of view.

Change the subject.
Politicians often do this. Say "I'm not here to talk about X. I think Y is a more important issue." To be more subtle, don't announce changing the subject, just do it. Segue into the answer you want to give.

Keep answers short.
The more you ramble on, the more opportunity exists for you to say the wrong thing. On uncertain ground, take very few, very small, very slow steps.

RELATED TOPICS

➤ Preparing for Interruptions, (pages 58–59)

➤ How to Present Bad News, (pages 62–63)

Inside Info

Colors and styles of clothing are very difficult to discuss without knowing exactly what you'll be wearing for your presentation and where you'll be wearing it. But a few general rules do apply.

Loud, bright colors are less professional than dark grey or blue, and brown is the least preferred color among professionals and executives.

The latest, wildest fashions are generally less acceptable than classic styles that aren't specifically associated with a particular year or season.

Dressing Appropriately

One of the greatest concerns about making a favorable impression while giving an important presentation is what to wear. Naturally, there is no simple answer. But there are guidelines to help you make an appropriate choice. They include:

1 Dress as nicely as, or nicer than, your audience. Women generally have more options than men, who should focus on conservative suits or, in less formal occasions, sports jackets and slacks. If you can't be sure, be safe by dressing a little more formally than you think is necessary. It's always easier to loosen up your tie or remove your jacket than to add one you didn't bring with you.

2 Stay neat and clean for the presentation. Make your last-minute adjustments—like tightening your tie, arranging your hair, or retouching your makeup—before you enter the presentation room.

3 Avoid worn shoes or cheap-looking briefcases, pens, watches, or other such accessories. Men should empty their pockets to achieve a better look.

WORDS TO LIVE BY

"You are only as good as the people you dress."

—Halston

Blending in

Pay attention to the clothing of the people around you. In your own organization, observe the wardrobes of your colleagues and those on and above the level to which you report. Select the clothing you'll wear for your presentation to blend in with what those in the audience will probably be wearing.

TimeSaver

Spend an evening going through your closet to find one or two optimal presentation outfits—including shoes, socks or stockings, and accessories—and look at yourself from all angles in a full-length mirror. When you find an outfit or two that look good, make sure they are comfortable by sitting, crossing your legs, and bending over. If the clothes pass these tests, then put these outfits aside. Top fashion editors recommend putting all the clothes on one hanger along with the tie or other accessories, so you'll have your presentation garb selected and ready to go. You'll then be free to consider other priorities on the morning of your presentation.

CASE IN POINT

As a finalist in the bid for a large architectural firm's printing, James Molina had honed his presentation to a fine tool. The night before the big meeting, he practiced in front of the mirror and hung his best suit out for the next day.

The following morning James was in a hurry to get there early and decided not to take the time to wash his hair or shine his shoes. His logic: He had a great presentation and a great suit—what more could he need?

As it turned out, plenty! James altogether overlooked the fact that architects are detailed-oriented souls. When they noticed his scuffed-up shoes and flakes of dandruff on the shoulders of his "great suit," they wondered if James could give their account the detailed attention it needed. In the end, they awarded the account to another printer.

RED ALERT!

Unless it's for a carefully planned effect—like the tuxedos worn by sports announcers at boxing events—overdressing for your presentation can be just as "gauche" as underdressing. It's a good idea to have at least one outfit in your wardrobe that's "multipurpose"—quality material, conservative cut, dark color—to fit in with any of the wide range of clothing selections you may encounter in an unknown audience.

RELATED TOPICS

➤ Likability and Credibility, (pages 66–67)

➤ Projecting a Favorable Persona, (pages 86–87)

Inside Info

Attitude is the key to likability and credibility not only because the audience picks up on your attitude almost instantly, but because your attitude gives subtle direction to a wide range of other clues you throw out to the audience.

Haughty, cold, or distant presenters are never well liked by their audiences. They also tend to be rated as less credible than down-to-earth, warm, and friendly presenters even though they exhibit the same general degree of expertise and knowledge.

Likability and Credibility

These two qualities are without question the underpinnings of a successful presentation.

Simply put, if your audiences doesn't like you—and, more important, doesn't trust you—they won't be receptive to what you have to say.

While separate and often unequal, these attributes are related to some of the same underlying aspects of your personality. To increase your likability and credibility for your next presentation, try paying more attention to:

Facial Expressions

Smiling is probably the most important facial expression for presenters, yet most people don't smile enough. To appear more likable and credible, you'll want to smile much more than you think you should.

Believe it or not, you can carry this *too* far. A simple rule is "don't smile all the time." For example, listen to questions, write on the chalkboard, shuffle through your notes, and work the presentation equipment without smiling. Then, when you do smile, it'll mean something favorable to your audience.

Tone of Voice

Unless you're a trained singer or actor, it's difficult to control your tone of voice directly, but you *can* influence it. For example, say a sentence while frowning and thinking a sad thought. Now say the same sentence while smiling and thinking a happy thought.

There's a difference in your tone of voice that your audience will instantly convert into higher likability ratings.

You can add credibility through your tone of voice in the same general way. But, in addition, you must cultivate a more certain attitude, not just a happy one. Uncertainty in your thoughts comes out in your voice, and this will undoubtedly lead the audience to assume that you're unknowledgeable about your topic.

RED ALERT! Any defensiveness, worry, uncertainty, or efforts to deceive will be noticed by the audience and immediately translated into relatively poor marks for likability and credibility. Be confident of what you're saying, and the audience will accept it with much less skepticism.

Body Language

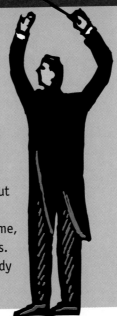

Sitting or standing, leaning forward or backward, slouching or poised for fast action, your body conveys a great deal of information that your audience translates into likability and credibility judgments.

Again, you can learn certain favored movements and postures, such as standing to make an important point or to emphasize your credibility, and keeping your hands and legs uncrossed to appear friendlier to the audience. But the shortcut is to maintain the proper mental attitude: confident, informed and informative, unpressed for time, and open to other people's ideas and suggestions. If you can train yourself to feel this way, your body language will take care of itself.

SKILL BUILDERS
Developing Audience Interaction

The supreme skill of successful presenters is to interact with the audience in a way that makes them feel happy, well cared for, and appreciated—even if you and they don't actually converse.

The interaction begins when you are introduced to your audience and make your opening remarks. It continues as you make your points, respond in subtle ways to the audience's facial expressions and body language, and deal with their questions and comments after the conclusion of your presentation.

RELATED TOPICS

➤ **Increasing Your Charisma, (pages 68–69)**

➤ **Effective and Ineffective Gestures, (pages 88–89)**

➤ **Body Language, (pages 90–91)**

We've talked about smiling in many other contexts, but the research makes it clear that charismatic leaders tend to smile more than dull ones.

Increasing Your Charisma

The dictionary defines *charisma* as a personal quality attributed to leaders who arouse popular devotion and enthusiasm. Obviously, it's easier to describe how it affects audiences than to say what it is.

Furthermore, charisma is an uncommon trait. If we all had it, it might cancel itself out, if only through excessive familiarity.

But even if we don't think we possess it ourselves, we can all recognize charisma when we feel it. And by studying the presentations of charismatic people, it's possible to discover ways to increase your own charismatic impact on your audiences.

Here are some tips to help you:

1 Be more animated when you give a presentation.

Put yourself mentally into a more active mode. Walk a little, gesture more broadly, use the whole stage or presentation area. Charismatic people expend more physical energy than average ones. The more animated you are, without becoming manic, the more chance you have to favorably influence your audience.

2 Be more outgoing and interactive with people.

Listen a little more eagerly when they talk to you. Respond a little more enthusiastically when you like what they say. Charismatic people make strong impressions on those they meet and interact with. Putting more expression into your listening and speaking will help you make a more favorable impression on your audience.

3   Let your voice use its whole range of communications capability.

Charismatic people are natural actors, using all their gifts to captivate and hold their audience's attention. Your voice is a unique tool for accomplishing this. Vary your volume from a whisper to a proud roar. Vary your tones from a dulcet question to an imperious command.

4   Don't hide your emotions.

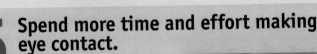

Let your voice, body language, gestures, and facial expressions reveal what you're truly feeling. Charismatic people know that human connections are made more easily on the emotional rather than the intellectual plane. That's why they readily share their emotions, and respond strongly to the emotions of others.

RED ALERT!

If you don't feel genuine about what you're doing, it's very easy to go over the top. That's why charisma is most effective when it emanates from honest feelings, honest interest in others, and honest efforts to make intrapersonal connections. If you overdo things to make a calculated impact, you risk sliding from charisma into caricature and what's closely associated with that—disrespect.

5   Spend more time and effort making eye contact.

Research shows that locking eyes with one person has a favorable impact on *all* the people in the group. Charismatic leaders use every means at their disposal—including expressive eye contact—to connect with their audiences in favorable and influential ways.

RELATED TOPICS

➤ Building Your Confidence, (pages 70–71)

➤ Body Language, (pages 90–91)

➤ Breathing and Voice Projection, (pages 94–95)

Building Your Confidence

Aside from experience, the best way to build confidence is through intensive preparation. You want to work on acquiring:

- extensive knowledge of the subject, so you can work with few notes and answer questions easily from memory.

- thorough reliance on the equipment so that you're comfortable working all the controls.

- sufficient experience in making the presentation to allay your nervousness and uncertainty.

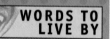

WORDS TO LIVE BY

"Early in life I had to choose between honest arrogance and and hypocritical humility. I choose honest arrogance and have seen no occasion to change."

—Frank Lloyd Wright

he best way to build your confidence for making presentations, of course, is to give some great presentations and get the positive feedback they earn you.

But until you have the opportunities to gain this confidence-boosting experience, it's good to be able to produce some at will. Here are few techniques that will help you feel and appear confident in front of your audience even when you're not:

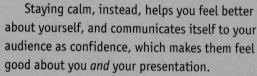

Stay Calm

Anxiety, hypertension, and stage fright not only make you feel bad but also reflect onto your audience and make them feel bad—about you *and* your presentation.

Staying calm, instead, helps you feel better about yourself, and communicates itself to your audience as confidence, which makes them feel good about you *and* your presentation.

To get calm and stay calm, take at least five deep, slow breaths. Close your eyes and visualize the air going into and out of your lungs as you breathe. Fill them all the way up, then empty them all the way out. Take at least 10 seconds for each in-breath and another 10 seconds for each out-breath. Repeat the sequence as necessary before you begin your presentation. You can even do it surreptitiously if you're in view of your audience while you're waiting to begin.

Remain Consistent

Confident presenters know the points they want to make to their audiences, and they work steadily toward them. They almost never alter their values, stated goals, points of view, factual statements, or interpretations of the situations they're discussing.

In the absence of self-confidence, you can at least emulate confident speakers by maintaining as much consistency as possible in *what* you present and *how* you present it.

TimeSaver

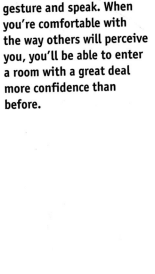

Practice your presentation in front of a mirror and pay special attention to your facial and body language as you gesture and speak. When you're comfortable with the way others will perceive you, you'll be able to enter a room with a great deal more confidence than before.

Appear Certain

It's always dangerous to pretend to be more certain of your facts—and interpretations of them—than you really are. It's just too easy to fall into dumb mistakes or a rigid attitude, either of which will quickly turn your audience against you.

The presenters can convince the audience that they are very certain of what they're saying, of what they believe, and of what they want their audiences to take away with them from a presentation.

You can therefore appear more confident than you really feel by at least being certain of what you're trying to communicate. The good thing about trying this tactic is that certainty not only helps you communicate confidence to your audience but also helps you to eventually build "the real thing."

RED ALERT!

Confidence should not be interpreted as arrogance or "cockiness," which is the quickest way to encourage the audience to shut down all eyes and ears. Because many people mask their fear or uncertainty with arrogance, it's important that you take special care to ensure that this undermining trait doesn't emerge during your presentation.

RELATED TOPICS

➤ Four Presentation Phobias and How to Overcome Them, (pages 78–79)

➤ Projecting a Favorable Persona, (pages 86–87)

Inside Info

Make sure to run the text of your presentation by a native speaker before you deliver it. This will help to ensure that nothing is lost in the translation or more important, that a word or phrase is not misinterpreted.

Presenting in a Foreign Language

Are you fluent in French? Spanish? German? Portuguese? Italian? Whatever your answer, you may be asked— or choose—to give a presentation to an audience that calls a foreign language its "native tongue."

Some people have a gift for learning foreign languages and have little or no trouble gaining enough command of a new language to deliver a well-rehearsed presentation and handle a few simple follow-up questions. But the rest of us can't get past "Where is the nearest bathroom?" and "How much does this cost?" in any language other than English.

Nevertheless, you can still give a successful presentation in a foreign language—even several different languages—if you handle things correctly. Let's look at how to get the job done.

2,8 t

Land- und forstwirtsch. Verkehr frei

Using Translators

The simplest way to get by in a foreign language is to have someone else do it for you. Outside the United States, people are far more comfortable with and prepared for language barriers than we are—and for several reasons.

First, there are many resource people available who can conduct detailed business conversations, discussions, and even negotiations in more than one language. So if you're speaking English, they can listen—and even ask questions—quite comfortably without you doing anything special.

In addition, the United Nations approach to "simultaneous translation" is relatively common at international presentations outside the United States. You speak into a microphone and a translator in a soundproof booth echoes your words in a foreign language into a microphone that broadcasts to foreign language audience members equipped with pocket radio receivers. In some situations, members of the audience can individually choose to hear your presentation in any one of several different languages.

This process of simultaneous translation, however, is not without its share of flaws and weaknesses. Colloquial expressions, jokes, "double entendres," and highly technical language often doesn't translate well. In addition, the person translating is often a sentence or so behind you,

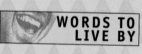

WORDS TO LIVE BY

"Life is a foreign language; all men mispronounce it."
—Christopher Morley

so the audience's reaction may be somewhat out of sync with what you're saying.

You can reduce these problems by speaking a little slower than normal and by giving your translator the text of your presentation in advance so that both of you can review any difficult or questionable passages.

Speaking the Language Yourself

Don't try this unless you have a facility for foreign languages, or you've studied one enough to feel comfortable making a presentation in it.

The best method is to get your text typed in phonetic form, so the words are spelled the way you're going to pronounce them. This minimizes your need to read and think in the foreign language and helps you sound more fluent to your audience.

RED ALERT!

It's vital to have your presentation vetted by someone who is completely fluent in the language you'll be using. This is the only way to ensure that there are no embarrassing phrases or inappropriate remarks inadvertently buried where you won't notice them—but your audience will.

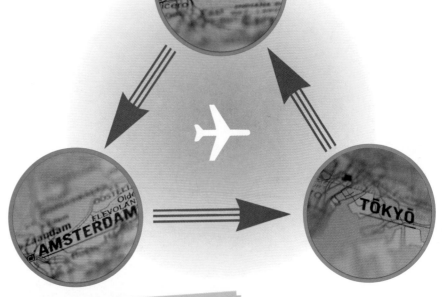

Travel Itinerary
- **Leave Chicago:** 4/5/96
- **Arrive Amsterdam:** 4/5/96
- **Leave Amsterdam:** 4/7/96
- **Arrive Tokyo:** 4/8/96
- **Leave Tokyo:** 4/11/96
- **Arrive Chicago:** 4/12/96

Meeting Itinerary
- **Chicago:** 4/5/96
- **Amsterdam:** 4/6/96
- **Tokyo:** 4/11/96
- **Chicago:** 4/13/96

SKILL BUILDERS
Rehearsing in a Foreign Language

Rehearsals are doubly important when you're presenting to an audience that doesn't speak your most fluent language. Practice what you'll be saying and the gestures and intonation you'll be using, so you can feel confident you're getting your message across regardless of the language barrier.

RELATED TOPICS

➤ **The Value of Rehearsals,** (pages 56–57)

Inside Info

As much as possible, it's best to take a statesman-like stance with the media. One good method is to pretend you're a presidential politician at the end of a long and illustrious career. You're full of confidence, war stories, and wisdom. It's generally a bad idea to let the media see you gloating over victories or spouting sour grapes over losses. In the same way, it usually reflects badly on you to criticize others by name or to make predictions about which you're not absolutely certain.

Print Media, TV, and Radio Interviews

With everyone getting their "fifteen minutes of fame," it's more and more likely you'll be interviewed by a reporter for a newspaper, magazine, TV, or radio show.

To them, the interviewee is nearly always a target, an object, a sitting duck they intend to use to fill their empty spaces with "spiffy" quotes or juicy tidbits that will attract and hold their own audience's attention.

That makes the interview a little bit of an adversarial action. So the rules that apply are quite different from those you follow when you're answering questions from ordinary members of your audience. There are some useful distinctions:

Stick to Your Own Message

Unlike ordinary members of your audience, most reporters and other media interviewers don't ask questions because they sincerely want to know the answers. Instead, they generally have a good idea of the answer you'll give before they ever ask the question. They ask questions either to:

- maneuver you into saying whatever the story or the show needs next.
- make themselves look good.
- put you on the spot.

Since this is nearly always the case, there's no reason for you to go quietly to the slaughter. Instead, use their questions merely as jumping-off points to get across your prepared message.

Answer Carefully

While you generally want to agree with ordinary members of your audience who ask questions, be far more careful before you agree with a proposition put to you by a member of the media. These queries nearly always come with far-reaching implications, assumptions, and generalizations—with which you may not entirely agree.

Instead, learn to begin your answers with phrases along the lines of: "No, I'd say it was more like . . ." or "That's not true, because . . ." or even "I can't agree with that. The facts show . . ."

Remember Your Impact

In a small room filled with colleagues you know and who know you, you can safely answer off the cuff or without much forethought, because there will be plenty of opportunities later on to expand on your answer or even take back something you said that was inaccurate.

But when you're interviewed by the media, remember that millions of viewers may be watching. You will seldom get a chance to rephrase, restate, or rescind what you've said before. So be extra vigilant. Think before you speak, and be very clear about your meaning. If it's possible for someone to misunderstand you, they probably will.

"I can't agree with that position because the research along with our internal studies shows . . ."

"On behalf of the Cynergetic Corporation, I'd like to announce the arrival of . . ."

RELATED TOPICS

➤ **Gauging the Language Style to Your Specific Audience, (pages 34–35)**

➤ **Preparing for Interruptions, (pages 58–59)**

➤ **Thinking on Your Feet, (pages 62–63)**

Managing Stress, Anxiety, and Fear

I n an old "Star Trek" episode, Captain Kirk was inadvertently split into two people by the Transporter. One copy was all emotion and drive, the other was all intellect and logic. Neither was much good without the other.

The interesting idea was that the raw emotion and drive had to channeled and controlled by the intellect and logic to create a knowledgeable, capable captain for the Starship Enterprise.

In the same way, the stress, anxiety, and fear you naturally feel in the hours, days, and weeks leading up to a presentation are *not* your enemies. They are among the most important elements you utilize in converting a bland, boring presentation into an exciting, memorable one.

That's why your goal is not to eliminate these feelings but to massage and control them in ways that actually benefit your presentation and performance.

Here are some tips on how to do so:

1 Don't fear the fear.
Roosevelt's words have never applied more perfectly than they do to making top-quality presentations. The problem is not that you feel stressed, anxious, or afraid but rather that you're *worried about experiencing* those feelings. Actually, they're very natural, and it would be inappropriate if you never experienced them!

Take time to reflect on the meaning of the "Star Trek" explanation at the beginning of this chapter and welcome your stress, anxiety, and fear, for they are the wellsprings that provide the power to make a truly great presentation.

Learning Simple Stress Management

For many, anxiety and stress become paralyzing factors. Practice the following stress relief exercises:

- Take in a deep breath through your nose, filling your lungs. Pause for a moment and release slowly, letting the breath out through your mouth. Repeat several times.
- Close your eyes and visualize a calmer environment, such as a favorite vacation spot or your backyard hammock. Try remembering how you felt and guide your mind to "think" yourself there again.

2 Find the source of the fear.

While it's natural to feel stress, anxiety, and fear, it's also natural for people to have such complex personalities that no two people will have precisely the same combination of those feelings for precisely the same reasons.

But knowing the source of your stress, anxiety, and fear is valuable because it brings those feelings into perspective and makes them more manageable.

One speaker, for example, may feel dread before a presentation because she's afraid a broken project switch will fail her during an important part of the presentation. Another will feel an equal level of anxiety because when he was a boy he drew a complete blank during a holiday recitation on the stage in front of the entire school and his family.

3 Channel the fear from source to resolution.

Knowing the source of of these feelings allows you to find a connection between it and its happy resolution. One speaker can simply buy a new projector switch, while the other can provide crib notes that guarantee he'll always know his next line.

By completing the connection between the source of your stress, anxiety, and fear and a satisfactory resolution, you create a wonderful, safe channel in which that energy can flow— controlled yet powerful enough to make a very positive impression on your audience.

RELATED TOPICS

➤ Building Your Confidence, (pages 70–71)

➤ Four Presentation Phobias and How to Overcome Them, (pages 78–79)

Inside Info

The best way to counter one or more of these phobias is not by direct frontal attack or by denial, repression, or force. Rather, the best remedy is to dive into and embrace the phobia as soon as possible, to explore it thoroughly, and to admit its existence within you. Only then can you begin to reduce its influence by experimenting with thoughts and feelings that intrinsically leave less room for the phobia.

In other words, first experience, then counter, your phobias with memories of good feelings you've experienced and with mental run-throughs of scenarios reflecting the future outcomes you can most reasonably expect.

WORDS TO LIVE BY

"Tell us your phobias and we will tell you what you are afraid of."

—Robert Benchley

Four Presentation Phobias and How to Overcome Them

In addition to the normal stress, anxiety, and fear you can expect before giving any presentation, there are four additional fears—more accurately referred to as phobias—which are so extreme, so powerful, and so unusual that they deserve separate mention as well as separate remedies.

These phobias involve the fear of failure, of success, of humiliation, and of attention. They sound innocuous enough, but to the sufferer any one of them can be worse than the innermost circle of Dante's Inferno.

Let's briefly examine each of these phobias, with an eye toward overcoming even the faintest tinge of any one you might feel.

Fear of Failure

Much more than simple anxiety over giving a presentation, fear of failure is a phobic reaction to the opportunity to do something new, exciting, and potentially important. In extreme cases, it can cause sufferers to sabotage their own opportunities.

A useful remedy is to think back on past successes, to develop and cherish the good feeling those memories usually engender, and to try to carry that good feeling with you into the presentation.

Fear of Success

The phobic reaction to success takes on two distinct forms: a person may be afraid to give a presentation in front of people who are already successful, or be afraid to gain a major success him- or herself.

You can overcome the fear of others by focusing on their overall humanity. As the saying goes, they shower, shave, and dress in the morning just like you do.

Your fear of your own potential success will often yield ground to happy thoughts of past successes and a general mental focus not on long-term consequences but on day-to-day activities in preparation for your presentation.

Fear of Humiliation

Human nature has little room for anything that deflates our ego or robs us of our self-esteem. If you knew this would happen in your next presentation, you'd be nuts to go through with it.

The secret is that you don't know this will happen, you're just *afraid* it might! This fear will generally fade and diminish if you instead refocus your attention on what is much more likely to happen and then rehearse sufficiently to minimize the real possibilities of public humiliation.

Fear of Attention

Stage fright is a simple form of this phobia. While a few people crave the limelight, most would rather watch than be watched. When fear of attention interferes with your ability to give a presentation, however, it requires remedial action.

One of the best techniques is to build up to your presentation in small stages. Take—even create—opportunities to speak in public or to be the temporary center of attention.

When you see that the sky doesn't fall in just because you went on stage, your phobia will begin to dissipate.

 RED ALERT! Fear can cause people to do strange things and, like dogs, sometimes "bite." Be cautious if you have the tendency to become aggressive or violent when fearful. If your buttons are pushed more easily in an uncomfortable situation, seek help to learn how you can best cope with this.

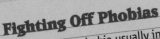 **Fighting Off Phobias**

The fright pattern of a phobia usually involves imagining dire consequences far above and beyond what a reasonable person would expect to occur. The remedy, therefore, is to focus on much more reasonable scenarios of what might happen and then to take reasonable precautions against them.

 **RELATED TOPICS**

▶ **Building Your Confidence,** (pages 70–71)

▶ **Dodging Your Poor Speaking Habits,** (pages 84–85)

The secret ingredient in a successful pitch to clients is the manner in which you respond to their unspoken needs. If your material responds to their questions or concerns *before* they have the opportunity to address them, you'll gain the advantage of "knowing what they want." Clues can be gathered from information culled from client's previous business dealings, body language, offhand conversation, and other clues you may pick up during this process.

WORDS TO LIVE BY

"Ya gotta do what ya gotta do."

—Sylvester Stallone (in *Rocky IV*)

Pitching to a Client

When you're trying to convince someone to let you help them with a special product, you face tougher obstacles than merely presenting your work. Your audience may range from one or more people who already admire your work and are inclined to take your advice, all the way to people you've never met who are also being pitched to by your competitors. Such diversity in the nature of your relationship with clients makes it imperative that you persuade them that your services are the ideal match for their product. To succeed, you must deliver a top-notch presentation utilizing several critical factors:

1 Act as if you already have the contract.

The number-one way to make a great presentation is to imagine that the potential client has already selected you to do the work. This means you should develop your ideas, create a few samples, work out a project plan, and cast the entire presentation not as "here's what we would do," but as "here's what we've begun doing."

This can be an expensive and time-consuming route to take, and it requires you to do a lot more homework and preparation than would be necessary for a simple presentation in which you're watching the budget. But it guarantees you'll make a great impression, and it puts the client in the position of *having to* reject you—emotionally much more difficult to do than not to accept you.

2 Sell them on yourself *and* what you're offering.

Whether or not the topic is listed in the agenda, one of the central items of interest will be *you*. Not just your organization, your team, and your presentation—but you personally.

The clients you pitch will be interested to know your personal background, attitude, knowledge, and capabilities. Although your life doesn't have to be the proverbial open book, people want to know who they'll be working with. If they like you, they'll move toward giving you the project you want to do for them; if they don't, they simply won't!

3 Speak to the dynamics of client decisions.

If client decisions were entirely predictable, those who pitch to them would have much easier lives. But don't worry: There's no danger of clients becoming predictable any time soon.

Instead of focusing on the strengths you're trying to pitch, your clients may focus on trivial matters or get bogged down in some idiosyncratic aspect of the presentation (one that you don't believe has significant impact on their decision). In many cases, the client may simply have a different vision for its organization than you're presenting.

If possible, find out what these details of your client's "agenda" are prior to your presentation—and then address them. If you don't, your presentation might ignore the very issues the client is most intent on.

RED ALERT!

Be wary of the client who asks you to present a detailed volume of work on spec.

Speculative ventures, whether in financial markets or in the visual communications industry, are full of risks. Organizations that choose to perform work on spec set themselves up to loose income and expenses. If you decide to pitch a job on spec (whether from a client or by entering a contest or competition), you may not be awarded the job and additionally may lose potential opportunities to bid on other, more lucrative assignments.

You're the best judge of how much risk you feel comfortable taking. Be sure to weigh both sides of the situation fairly. As a rule, every organization should create a policy on the acceptance of speculative assignments taking into consideration both the risks and benefits and the company's own financial situation.

> "We like your work, but we'd like to see a few ideas before we award the contract."

> "We're not really sure of the overall direction on this account. Can you give us a few ideas for direction along with the contract bid?"

TimeSaver

Sometimes, there's a "brother-in-law" with the inside track to the client. If so, nothing short of a miracle will make your presentation match your aspirations. After a few such presentations, you may decide you don't want to butt heads with any more literal or figurative brothers-in-law. To help identify "no-win" situations, try to "qualify" your audiences before you agree to give a presentation by asking why they want you to present, who else they're asking, and what criteria they'll use to make their choice.

RELATED TOPICS

➤ Building Excitement into Your Presentation, (pages 38–39)

➤ The First Five Minutes, (pages 82–83)

➤ Breathing and Voice Projection, (pages 94–95)

The First Five Minutes

magine that you're standing in front of a powerful business leader with your presentation to sell. He or she fixes you with a stare and says firmly "You've got five minutes!" It's an Arrid Extra Dry moment, to be sure—unless you're ready.

The one thing an experience like this teaches is that you always have only five minutes with an audience—the *first* five minutes. It's during this initial period that you make your primary impression on them, capture or lose their interest in you and your topic, and set the stage for their later acceptance—or rejection—of your purpose in making the presentation.

That's why you won't go wrong if you prepare every presentation as though you have only this critical five-minute period to win your audience's permission to continue. Here's what you should put into those first five minutes of every presentation.

WHO YOU ARE

Even assuming you have the best motivation and the most important information for helping your audience with this presentation, they'll still want to know about the source of the information. Are you credible? Will you be easy to work with? Do you follow through? You're asking the audience to invest their time and attention in you. Give them reasons to trust you and have confidence in your judgment.

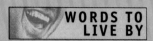

WHAT YOU KNOW

Work in some information about your background—perhaps anecdotes about your past adventures and, most important, successes—or a straight-forward listing of your relevant credentials and experience.

Following the Five-Minute Rule

Keep polishing those first five minutes of your presentation. While you're delivering them, and afterward, review how well the audience reacts and receives them. You'll find that you can use your most successful first five minutes—or at least the basic pattern of them—over and over again in nearly every presentation you give.

MAIN PURPOSES

Before you've talked more than a few minutes, you should make clear to your audience exactly why you're making this presentation, and why you're making it to *them* instead of some other audience.

MAIN IDEAS

Your introductory remarks should contain a riveting and powerful explanation of the nature of your topic, why it's important, and what your audience will learn by listening to the rest of your presentation.

`03:00`   `04:00`   `05:00`

WHAT YOU WANT FROM THE AUDIENCE

It's critical to set the audience straight regarding what you're hoping they will do when you've finished your presentation.

RELATED TOPICS

➤ **Preparing for Interruptions,** (pages 58–59)

➤ **Thinking on Your Feet,** (pages 62–63)

Dodging Your Poor Speaking Habits

"UM"

Regardless of topic, experience, or venue, there are some poor speaking habits that can easily creep into and take hold of a presenter's style. Once they do, these unintentional habits can zap half the strength from your delivery, and the impact on your audience is significantly diminished.

Here's what to watch out for:

Hiding Behind a Lectern

If possible, use a special lectern with such a flimsy base that you can't hang on to it. Why? Because standing behind a lectern lessens your impact on your audience and limits your ability to use your body language most effectively. Instead, stand clear. Move around. And see how much better your audience reacts to your presentation.

Filling Every Void

As part of the media generation, nearly everyone watches too much TV and film. Accustomed to such a constant influx of sound, we tend to feel there's no room in a presentation for silence. But, quite the contrary, filling every void is both unnecessary *and* undesirable. The white spaces created around your text and graphics are vitally important to the readability and impact of the visual presentation. In the same way, silence—between your words (and possibly your sound effects)—can be as important as the words themselves.

Learn the art of making a point and then giving the audience a few moments for it to sink in. It's not necessary to fill every second of your presentation with sound.

Monotony

The human voice is capable of such a wide range of expressions that to talk in a monotone is almost an offense against Nature! Talk into a tape recorder and listen to yourself until you feel comfortable varying your tone, pitch, volume, and pace. Practice adding variety not only to your voice but also to your overall movement, body language, gestures, and facial expressions.

No Structure

The human mind craves structure. Just as we want stories to have a beginning, a middle, and an end, we want presentations to start off with premises and background, and then to proceed through facts and illustrations toward conclusions and ramifications. If you don't give your presentation a perceptible structure, you're likely to leave your audience fundamentally dissatisfied.

Rambling

Many people can talk for hours and hours about your topic. That's not your job. Your audience wants—and deserves—a succinct presentation. To deliver one, review your early drafts and find tighter, more accurate ways to express your points. Eliminate all the ideas and anecdotes you don't really need. This should help to ensure that your presentation proceeds in a direct line without unnecessary rambling.

Reading

Unless you're reading the exact words you would naturally say to your audience, there's a major difference in emotion, energy, and influence between a presentation you deliver extemporaneously from your heart and one you read from a manuscript with your eyes. That's why you're much better off jotting brief notes on some index cards and using them to jog your memory, point by point.

RED ALERT! Nothing can turn an audience off faster than a presentation filled with nervous utterings of "um, you know," etc. Prepare for your presentation by speaking into a tape recorder and then listening to the recording. Note any uncomfortable pauses or "ums," and then practice eliminating them during rehearsal.

TimeSaver
After you become aware of your bad speaking habits, briefly list them on an index card and place the card on the lectern where you can occasionally glance at it. By doing so, you will be periodically reminded of what *not* to do.

RELATED TOPICS

➤ Building Your Confidence, (pages 70–71)

➤ Projecting a Favorable Persona, (pages 86–87)

➤ Breathing and Voice Projection, (pages 94–95)

Inside Info

Although a bit of acting plays into every successful presentation, remember that your audience is comprised of potential clients who will likely be doing business with you if your presentation is successful. So don't put up such a false front that your real self pales in comparison.

Projecting a Favorable Persona

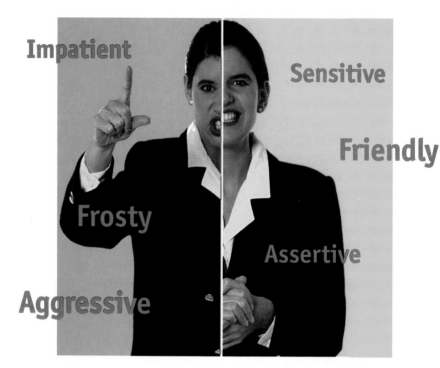

The core of a great presentation is *you*—the presenter. If people like and respect you, generally they'll accept and approve your material. But if they dislike or distrust you, your material will not find a welcome audience.

That's why it's critical to avoid giving the wrong signals to your audience from the minute you come into their sight until the minute you leave. Pay particular attention to controlling anything that smacks of the characteristics discussed on the next page.

SKILL BUILDERS

Building a Persona

A presentation is a performance, so it's important to develop an outward "character" who does the presenting. This person should be outgoing, good-humored, patient, and warm toward others. If this doesn't describe your present personality, make a conscious effort to cultivate the same persona as you see exhibited by other good presenters. This will save you a lot of problems and win supporters as you move through not only your presentation but the rest of your life.

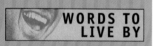

WORDS TO LIVE BY

"Once you get the right image the details aren't that important."
—Abbie Hoffman

A Bad Attitude

This is a very broad category. It includes any hint that you might be haughty or overbearing, pompous or frosty, impatient or anxious, insensitive to others, or unwilling to compromise.

Any personal attitude that's generally perceived as a negative one has a magnified impact on an audience who senses it in a presenter. That's why it's important to maintain a smiling face, an easygoing demeanor, and a warm heart at all times in front of your audience.

An Aggressive Stance

Aggressiveness—distinct from assertiveness—is another broad category of signals that presenters should never display to their audiences.

Simply defined, *assertiveness* is merely a method of looking out for your own interests, while *aggressiveness* is a method of pursuing your own interests even at the expense of others.

In this category of signals to avoid is included any hint of racism or sexism, hostility toward other individuals or groups, generalized anger, personal or group insults, or any behavior that might indicate your feeling of superiority over others.

A Closed Mind

Audiences generally take very badly to presenters who aren't willing to listen to criticism or suggestions, who jump to conclusions about what others are trying to say, who refuse to discuss certain factors or topics, and who seem to know all the answers before the questions are even formulated.

You'll make a much better impression on your audience if you cultivate an open attitude, a willingness to listen patiently while others explain their ideas and views, and a good-natured tolerance of suggestions—even if you can easily show others they have no merit.

RED ALERT! Don't try to come up with excuses if your audience sees you lose your temper or otherwise behave in a negative way. Be professional, apologize, and then move on. By dwelling on the unfriendly moment, you'll only reinforce it in the audience's mind.

RELATED TOPICS

➤ **Effective and Ineffective Gestures, (pages 88–89)**

➤ **Body Language, (pages 90–91)**

➤ **Eye Contact, (pages 92–93)**

The biggest problem presenters have in making effective gestures is that they limit their movements. Men may put their hands in their pockets; women may hold on to their arm with the other hand or may keep both their elbows unnaturally close to the body.

Get in the habit of leaving your arms comfortably hanging straight down until they have the urge to move. Then let them do so naturally. Step lightly from one foot to the other, even take a few steps, to add to the power of your gestures.

WORDS TO LIVE BY

"Handshaking is friendly until your hands bleed."

—Ralph G. Martin

Effective and Ineffective Gestures

Gestures like this demonstrate seriousness and a willingness to listen.

Gestures like this are used to explain a point or illustrate a situation.

The content of your presentation is only a small factor in the total impact you have on your audience. A much larger factor involves your gestures.

Like an actor, your job as presenter is to add the kind of gestures that will have the desired effect on your audience while keeping them fresh enough to take in the "meat" of your presentation.

Fortunately, this is fairly easy to accomplish. Just let your gestures be one outlet for your body's natural nervous energy. Instead of jiggling one foot or twirling a pencil in your fingers, make larger-than-normal gestures. Put your energy into them, and you'll find that your anxiety dissipates and your effectiveness with your audience increases.

Don't rehearse specific gestures for specific points in the presentation. Instead, concentrate on developing a repertoire of gestures that you'll use in your presentation as naturally and spontaneously as you use everyday gestures in your normal conversations.

After a while, whenever the situation warrants it, you'll be able to "switch gears" from everyday gestures to the larger, more dramatic presentation gestures without even knowing it.

Your repertoire of gestures should include many things.

You can use:

Smaller Upper Body Motions

1 Just as television actors learn to use tiny facial muscles to convey emotion when the TV camera is close up, presenters must learn to tone down their gestures when speaking to a small audience. Although you'll want to be conscious of your gestures, they shouldn't be much "louder" than if you were speaking with a few close friends. Notice how your head, hand, and arms move naturally in conversation and learn how to use them to naturally express your points.

Stronger, More Definite Gestures

2 Gentle, subtle motions are much easier for an audience of one to interpret than for an audience of one hundred. To spread your impact over the larger group, you'll have to work to boost your energy level and make proportionally stronger, faster, and more decisive gestures.

In general, these gestures tend to be a little more exaggerated than day-to-day conversational ones, with more movement of the elbows and upper arms, more angular action to head motions, and slightly larger movements of the eyes, eyebrows, eyelids, lips, and other facial muscles to compensate for the greater distances and more difficult sight lines your larger audiences must endure.

SKILL BUILDERS

Practicing Gestures

Practice in front of a mirror or videotape your presentation. Be sure to use the gestures appropriate to speaking in front of a large audience. Watch how particular gestures manifest themselves, and get comfortable with the motions. The more you practice, the more quickly they will become a natural part of your presentation package.

RELATED TOPICS

➤ **Projecting a Favorable Persona, (pages 86–87)**

➤ **Body Language, (pages 90–91)**

At one time, scientists thought that each move of the body in conversation or presentation had a specific meaning—much like words. It was assumed that you could simply read the sequence of meanings from a person's body language and know exactly what he or she was thinking.

Today, we know this kind of mechanistic thinking is probably inaccurate. Social scientists and communications specialists now claim that body language provides more of a background tone to a conversation or presentation than an item-by-item message. Study the body language of presenters and leaders you admire, and match your style as appropriate.

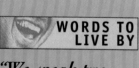

WORDS TO LIVE BY

"We speak two languages, one of which is verbal."
—Steve Rubenstein

Body Language

Body language has become a secondary language in most social situations. From dating to job interviews, people are becoming increasingly aware of the ways their bodies express their true feelings.

By understanding the expressive nature of the human body, you can adjust your body language to convey the message you want your audience to receive. In turn, your body language can be the deciding factor between delivering a mediocre presentation and an outstanding one. Two of the ways to make a big difference include:

1 Confidence

An expert presenter understands the importance of keeping the body very still at certain times. While you're waiting your turn to present, unnecessary movement can easily be interpreted by the audience as fidgeting, nervousness, distraction, lack of interest in the proceedings, or disdain for those in attendance. During your presentation, unnecessary movements only detract from the impact of the points you're trying to convey.

To project stillness, it's important to "absorb"—that is, not express—about 90 percent of the body movements you might normally make. Any movements you do initiate should be slow and deliberate.

Expressing Body Language

Practice your stillness in front of a mirror. Resist the initial urge to touch, scratch, pick at, or move anything. When you're first attempting this exercise, you might become irritated by extra sensations of itching and twitching. This quickly passes, and soon you'll be able to sit or stand very quietly in front of an audience.

RED ALERT! Avoid an image of weakness. As soon as you show any signs of using defensive body language, you establish yourself as someone with relatively little power or authority. So don't cross your arms in front of your body. Don't avert your face —or even your eyes—from those conversing with you. Don't hold both hands up, palms out, either chest high as if to shield your face or with your arms outstretched pointing like the hands of a clock showing 4:40 or 9:15.

There are many more defensive postures, of course, and with a little thought and practice you can avoid using most or all of them during your presentations.

2 Power and Authority

A sense of power and authority flows automatically from confidence, and with the right body language you can very easily enhance the sense of power and authority you project.

Above all, aim toward accentuating your positive body language. Without using any threatening gestures, you can project power and authority by maintaining a relaxed body posture while seated, but an erect body posture while standing. Keep your weight evenly balanced on both legs. As you walk, you can lengthen your strides by about 5 percent and walk a little faster than usual.

RELATED TOPICS

➤ Increasing Your Charisma, (pages 68–69)

➤ Effective and Ineffective Gestures, (pages 88–89)

➤ Eye Contact, (pages 92–93)

Don't make eye contact with someone on the left, then someone on the right, then someone at the back, then someone up front in your audience. All these years, you've probably been told to do it wrong, right?

It's far more effective to roam the audience with your eyes and spot the people agreeing with you: nodding, smiling, making facial expressions that validate yours or that indicate they've experienced the joy or pain you're discussing.

Make eye contact with these people, and keep coming back to them for more eye contact throughout your presentation.

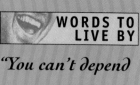

WORDS TO LIVE BY

"You can't depend on your eyes when your imagination is out of focus."

—Mark Twain

Eye Contact

Whether the eyes truly are the windows to the soul or just an extremely expressive feature of the human face, there's no doubt that your ability to make and use eye contact can be an important skill for increasing the impact and persuasive power of your presentations.

In smaller presentations, eye contact will not only increase your audience's perception of your warmth, friendliness, and intelligence but will also enable you to obtain useful feedback on how each audience member is receiving your presentation: favorably or unfavorably, agreeably or disagreeably, with an open or closed mind, and so on.

In larger presentations, eye contact serves as a vital tool for avoiding the dehumanizing influences of longer sightlines, voice amplification, and other aspects of bigger presentation venues.

To be effective with eye contact, make sure you're:

1 Confident in the knowledge of your material so that you can use your eyes to study your audience while you conduct your presentation.

 RED ALERT! Don't get caught staring. Many presenters miss the point of eye contact and stare endlessly into people's eyes, making others downright uncomfortable. Staring is *not* considered eye contact, and some view it as downright intimidating and confrontational.

2 Able to see well enough to make eye contact at the normal distances to members of your audience.

3 Familiar enough with body language signals that you can more easily spot people who are getting positive information and feelings from your presentation.

Making Eye Contact

Making brief eye contact with people who appear to be enjoying or agreeing with you, and continually coming back to them, is a great way to amplify the impact of your presentation.

Experience shows that warmth, persuasiveness, and the power of this eye contact greatly improve how these audience "allies" and others receive the presentation. What's more, their eye contact with you gives you the strength, courage, and enthusiasm to put more energy into your presentation—energy that others in the audience can feel and respond to.

RELATED TOPICS

➤ **Increasing Your Charisma,** (pages 68–69)
➤ **Body Language,** (pages 90–91)

Get more impact from your voice by using your whole range. Practice your presentations while you exaggeratedly vary your tone of voice, pitch, volume, and pace. By practicing the extremes—pleading and commanding, soprano and bass, whispering and shouting, speed-talking, and slow-mo—you increase the variability and power that's available to you without thinking during your presentations.

Breathing and Voice Projection

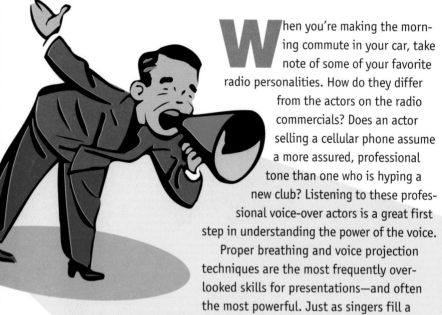

When you're making the morning commute in your car, take note of some of your favorite radio personalities. How do they differ from the actors on the radio commercials? Does an actor selling a cellular phone assume a more assured, professional tone than one who is hyping a new club? Listening to these professional voice-over actors is a great first step in understanding the power of the voice. Proper breathing and voice projection techniques are the most frequently overlooked skills for presentations—and often the most powerful. Just as singers fill a nightclub or concert hall with beautiful music, you can use your voice to perform in whatever presentation venue you're given. Here are some of the skills you need:

Practice Relaxation

Very few good things happen when your muscles are tense. Great physical performances—including making presentations—are much more likely to happen when you're relaxed. Good breathing is the key to relaxation.

To get relaxed and stay relaxed, take at least five deep, slow breaths. Close your eyes and visualize the air going into and out of your lungs as you breathe. Fill them all the way up, then empty them all the way out. Take at least ten seconds for each in-breath and another ten seconds for each out-breath. Repeat the sequence as necessary before you begin your presentation. If you're in view of your audience while you're waiting to begin, you can even do this exercise surreptitiously.

Develop Power

Your voice is one of the main instruments of your mind. You can use it to persuade, cajole, berate, and otherwise create emotional reactions when expressing yourself. But, like other parts of the human body, your voice thrives with constant, healthy use.

"Keep breathing."
—Sophie Tucker

So practice developing power in your voice. Start with raw power, the ability to project your voice over a greater distance. Volume is part of this skill, but so is filling your chest with air and resonating your voice with your mouth open wider than usual.

Think about the person ten feet, then twenty feet, then thirty feet away from you, and so on. See that person. Talk to that person, and you will develop more power in your voice.

SKILL BUILDERS

Breathing as a Prelude to Speaking

Breathing is "the essential skill" according to many excellent speakers. Breathe slowly and meditatively before you begin relaxing your body and your mind. Breathing regularly during your presentation can help your pacing and can greatly aid in controlling runaway emotions. Breathing more powerfully at well-chosen moments can also give your voice extra impact at a distance of as much as thirty yards!

RELATED TOPICS

▶ Dodging Your Poor Speaking Habits, (pages 84–85)

▶ Projecting a Favorable Persona, (pages 86–87)

Inside Info

Be very selective in the jokes you decide to tell, making sure they're in the context of your presentation. Some comedians are funny just because of their delivery—their accents, facial expressions, gestures, or whatever. Don't try to imitate these pros unless you're confident you can do it well. Instead, pick jokes that are funny on their own merit.

Using Humor

A good sense of humor—or at least a cheerful disposition—is almost a prerequisite for success as a presenter, which is why so many books offer jokes and light-hearted opening lines for would-be speakers.

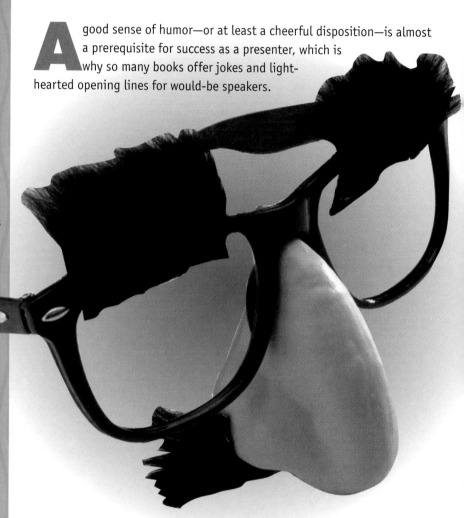

WORDS TO LIVE BY

"Analyzing humor is like dissecting a frog. Few people are interested and the frog dies of it."

—E. B. White

Here are several ways your sense of humor can be used to improve your presentations:

1 To break the ice

After a segment of your presentation heavy with meaning or complex thinking, tell a simple joke. You'll lighten the mood and provide welcome relief to your audience—and yourself.

2 To build audience rapport

Early in your presentation, and several times within it, tell a joke to share a laugh with your audience. People who laugh together tend to trust and feel better about each other. Also, studies have shown that people in a jovial mood are more open to new ideas, concepts, and changes.

RED ALERT! Never use humor to offend or belittle anyone. Avoid getting a laugh through any hints of racist or sexist mocking, anything offensive or "off-color," or anything that relies on shock value rather than simple surprise. You'll lose far more audience support than you'll gain through these tactics.

3 To show your vulnerability

You can win your audience's hearts and bridge the gap by telling a joke that gets a laugh at your own expense. Talk about a mistake you made early in your career, or something embarrassing that happened to you. Your vulnerability will bring the audience into your corner.

"This morning, while I was rehearsing for this presentation, I caused some damage. I was . . ."

★ SKILL BUILDERS — Assessing the Uses of Humor

Nothing falls flatter than a badly told joke. But no one is born a bad teller of jokes: There are only people who haven't tried hard enough at telling jokes well. Realize that jokes don't always have a punch line. Sometimes the best way to inject laughter into a presentation is with a funny aside or a wry observation. Gauge yourself with friends to see if you're a joke-telling type or if you're simply better at tossing a witty remark here and there. Bottom line: A forced joke is *not* funny!

RELATED TOPICS

➤ **Increasing Audience Interaction,** (pages 20–21)

➤ **Likability and Credibility,** (pages 66–67)

Inside Info

One of the best ways to evaluate yourself as a presenter is to view a video tape made from the audience's perspective. Some presentations are automatically videotaped, and you can often ask for a copy of the tape and view it at your convenience.

Other times, with prior permission, you can bring your own video camera and recorder, with a tripod, and set it up unobtrusively in the back of the room to capture your actual performance. Or, better yet, have someone operate it while you make your presentation. Even if the quality of the sound is bad and you sometimes walk out of the picture, a videotape is very accurate evidence of how well you put over your presentation on that particular day.

Analyzing Your Presentation

One of the best ways to improve your presentation skills and effectiveness is to analyze each presentation after it's complete. Some presenters—and various organizations that arrange for presenters—routinely distribute questionnaires that ask audience members to rate the speaker on his or her delivery, command of the material, personality, impact, use of visuals, responsiveness to the audience, and more. If you can get a look at your audience's responses to such a questionnaire, you'll learn a great deal about how to improve your presentation skills.

Even without this kind of formal questionnaire, you can work alone or with friends who have experienced your presentation to perform your own post presentation evaluation.

Of course, you'll consider the factors mentioned above. You should also consider other issues such as:

- How clearly your information came across to your audience
- How well you fit your presentation into the allotted time
- How confident you felt in giving the presentation
- How smooth and self-assured you appeared during your presentation
- Your personal bearing
- Your voice and body language
- The content of your presentation
- How well the audience responded
- What type of questions you were asked
- How well the equipment and venue suited and served your presentation

As you consider each of the items, your evaluation process should follow very simple lines. Specifically:

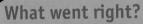

"Reorganizing my outline sure helped when . . ."

What went right?

This is where you pat yourself on the back. Did you say something witty that was well received? Did your audience ask all the appropriate questions following your presentation? Evaluating what went right is the best way to ensure that you'll be able to deliver another effective presentation.

After the relief of completing the presentation, most people are just excited to be done—even if the results were negative. Be honest with yourself. If the presentation didn't go well, or you simply fell on your face, examine the reasons. Dishonesty in introspection is a primary reason presenters fail again and again, because they simply refuse to examine and then learn from their mistakes.

"I guess I shouldn't have made that joke about . . ."

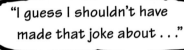

What went wrong?

Here, you ask yourself all the hard questions—and don't be surprised if you don't have all the answers. Sometimes what went wrong is hard to decipher. Did you present too much information and bore the audience? Did you offer incorrect or incomplete information? By breaking down your presentation into smaller elements, you'll be better able to "cure" the ills of your speech and give a better one next time.

What can I do better next time?

You can always do better next time, even if your presentation was a bit hit. Combine the "rights" with the "wrongs" and examine your presentation, segment by segment. If you're fortunate enough to have received feedback from the audience, integrate this information. Making an effective presentation is both an art and a science. Most important, they both take time and practice.

➤ Achieving Your Presentation Goals, (pages 10–11)

➤ The Day After, (pages 100–101)

The Day After

If there were one or two critical people sitting in on your presentation, you should consider giving them a phone call the following day to see how they enjoyed it and to find out if you can answer any questions.

This "hands-on" type of follow-up is the quickest and most effective way of getting what you want from a presentation and also helps you to develop vital working relationships.

You can increase your effectiveness by following up after your presentation with anything from a thank-you note to a comprehensive mailing of detailed reference material.

Let's look at some specifics:

1 If your objective was to entertain, amuse, or otherwise help one or more persons enjoy themselves, there's little need for follow-up. At most, you might want to send a thank you note or some other token of your appreciation for the audience.

BEGINNING MONDAY

Send out thanks to Jana for inviting me to speak.

Remember to mail out my background notes to V.P. of marketing.

2 If your objective was to convey critical information to your audience, the right kind of follow-up can help to convey even more information, or support the information you conveyed in your presentation. It's often a good idea to get in touch with your audience members, either as a group or individually, and offer to answer any additional questions or provide any further information they may desire.

3 If your objective was to persuade one or more persons of something important, you'll probably want to follow up to find out whether your persuasion was effective. You can do this either by asking directly or by monitoring whatever results would flow from persuasion. For example, if you make a presentation in support of a bond issue, a vote to pass the bond issue would be an indication that your presentation was indeed persuasive. A rejection of the bond issue, on the other hand, would make you ware that your presentation approach needs some modification next time.

TimeSaver
Consider distributing postcards or mailing-list forms after the presentation for those individuals who want more information. Leave a drop box by the door where they can immediately leave the cards after they've been filled out. Make sure to respond to these inquiries immediately.

Memoranda

9 AM

10 Call Jim Gates at Comco. See if he needs supplemental materials.

11

12

Thursday

9

EVENING

Friday

Talk to Jim, Christa, Evie and Fred—find out how they thought things went. Did I get the my message across?

EVENING

aturday
follow-up postcards members—need m Jana!

EVENING

4 If your objective was to motivate one or more persons into taking a specific action, you'll probably be interested in following up to press further for the action you want. Since you're the one who wants something done in this situation, it becomes your responsibility to contact the people in your audience. Sure, they have your telephone number, but if they're not motivated enough to act the way you want them to, they probably won't call to tell you so.

5 If your objective was to improve your image and credibility in the mind of one or more persons, you'll want to check back sometime in the future—perhaps as soon as a week or so, perhaps not for several months or even a year. You'll also want to have a good reason to get in touch with your audience again. But your real agenda will be simply to get a reading on your image and credibility, based on how the audience members treat you.

RELATED TOPICS

➤ Achieving Your Presentation Goals, (pages 10–11)

➤ Analyzing Your Presentation, (pages 98–99)

Glossary

Anxiety—A natural mix of feelings of anticipation, fear, and worry that most presenters experience in the days, hours, and minutes before they begin. Anxiety causes adrenaline to flow, and with practice you can use this adrenaline boost to give even more effective presentations.

Argument—The process of logically sequencing your information and ideas so as to bring the audience from their current attitudes or beliefs to new ones that you want to leave with them. Also, a discussion in which people are proposing different attitudes and beliefs.

Audience interaction—A process of increasing audience interest and satisfaction by asking questions, playing games, allowing input, and other related activities.

Audience size—A critical factor in preparing a presentation. The expected size of the audience dictates not only what equipment you'll need to make your presentation accessible to the audience but also how dense you can make your presentation and how much audience involvement you can anticipate.

Clip art—Professionally drawn generic cartoons, signs, illustrations, and other graphical material made available at low prices for unlimited use within presentations. Good selections of clip art can give any presentation a much more professional appearance, replace long text passages with vivid visuals, and increase the audience's overall interest level.

Contingencies—Fairly standard situations that can develop during any presentation and thus require preparation prior to the presentation. Three important contingencies include: Your audience is not interested in your topic, your audience wants much more information on your topic, and you're not allotted enough time to complete your presentation.

Credibility—Literally, the degree to which your audience accepts and believes what you say. It is enhanced by credentials, experience, facts, references, and attitudes.

Culture—The societal values, habits, attitudes, and behaviors that strongly determine how your audience accepts your presentation and reacts to it. Different nations, regions, and corporations all have different cultures.

Density—In a presentation, the ratio of hard information and difficult concepts to generalities, ordinary conversation, transitional material, jokes, and other "filler." The greater the density of information, the more difficult it is for your audience to follow and absorb the totality of your presentation material.

Distraction—Anything that tends to detract your audience's attention away from the point you're making or the message you're conveying. Distractions can be found everywhere—from sunlight glaring in through an open window to noisy audiovisual equipment to cocktail waitresses in skimpy clothing.

Dynamics—The group process within your audience that determines who sets the tone, who makes the decisions, and whose opinions are most important.

Focus—The extent to which all your information is organized and sequenced to convey and explain one or more main points. The more information supporting fewer points, the more "focus" you have in your presentation.

Handout—Formatted information related to your presentation that is given to your audience, generally on paper. Handouts can be gleaned directly from your presentation or can provide additional supporting information.

Headline—A brief, interesting, and generally summarizing statement of material about to be presented. You should include headlines in your presentation not only to keep your audience alert and interested but also to help them grasp your organization and arrangement of the content.

Language—The choice of words, structure, and expression included in your presentation. Aside from English, French, or some other language, you can and should be aware of your selection regarding other factors such as the formality or informality of your language and nonverbal body language.

Marker board—A vertical surface made to write on and then easily erase. They are very useful for showing computations, illustrating ideas, and conveying information when making presentations to smaller groups.

Multimedia—Modern technology for making presentations that includes computerized use of sound and visuals—everything from slide shows to animation and full-motion skits—to make your content more understandable and interesting.

Overdressing—Refers to dressing perhaps more formally than necessary. A good habit to cultivate, particularly if you're making presentations to strangers. Besides eliminating any danger of embarrassment, being the best-dressed person in the room gives you and your presentation a little more authority and credibility.

Overhead projector—A useful and reliable device for projecting any transparency onto a large screen where hundreds of audience members can view it comfortably. The transparencies can be hand drawn as you talk, printed in advance, or generated by a computer and then displayed on a special transparent screen designed for use with an overhead projector.

Pacing—The rate at which you convey information in your presentation. Ideally, you'll vary your pacing to fit the density of your material and the mood and attention span of your audience.

Pitching—The process of trying hard to convince your audience to take action on a specific idea or proposal you believe is a good one.

Planning—A critical aspect in the success of any presentation. Planning should cover content, organization, audiovisual materials and equipment, room setup, and rehearsal of your spoken words. The only reliable substitute for planning is experience in giving the same presentation to similar audiences.

Podium—A stable platform designed to hold papers, microphones, and other paraphernalia for a presenter who is standing up instead of sitting down. Holding onto a podium or standing motionless behind one tends to rob you and your presentation of energy and excitement.

Pointer—Any device that allows you to extend your reach to point out items on a large board or projection screen. Once long, straight sticks, today's pointers tend to be hand-held "laser beam" projectors.

Rapport—A strong relationship that the presenter develops with an audience through proper selection and use of language, content, attitude, and information. Good rapport with an audience can often overcome many other presentation shortcomings and mistakes.

Readability—A measure of how easy it is to understand the content of your presentation. Generally measured in terms of school "grade levels," readability goes up as you use bigger words, longer sentences, and more complex sentence structures.

Rhetoric—The art and study of using language effectively and persuasively. It involves many aspects of vocabulary, sentence structure, and thought processes.

Suspense—The use of hints about interesting things to come that keeps an audience attentive during a presentation.

Tickler—A system used to remind yourself of important points that you want to make in your presentation. The most common use of this system is writing notes on index cards.

Trust—The feeling of confidence and authority your audience gains from watching and listening to you. The more trust they feel, the more readily they will accept the content of your presentation.

Resources

Associations and Websites

American Marketing Association: http://www.ama.org/
Offers links to member sites and marketing newsgroups, access to info centers, conferences, directories, on-line services, and industry publications.

Interactive Services Association: http://www.isa.net/isa
This site promotes the development of consumer interactive services world-wide. Users can connect through it directly to Web sites of many of its members and can also get information on ISA conferences and public policy initiatives and answers to most frequently asked questions about on-line services.

Useful Organizations and Societies: http://www.ntu.ac.sg/~ctng/assoc.htm
One of the most comprehensive and up-to-date directories of major business, scientific, engineering, and educational societies on the Web. Very high quality.

Yahoo Business Organizations: http://www.yahoo.com/Business_and_ Economy/Organizations/
Best and most link-heavy directory of business organizations. Over twelve organizational categories including business development, consortia, foundations, professional organizations, and international trade, with brief descriptions at each listing.

Books

Communicate with Confidence. Dianna Booher. New York: McGraw-Hill, 1994.

Effective Presentation Skills: A Practical Guide for Better Speaking. Steve Mandel. Los Altos, Calif.: Crisp Publications, Inc., 1987.

Everything You Need to Know to Talk Your Way to Success. Burton Kaplan. Englewood Cliffs, N.J.: Prentice-Hall, 1995.

Executive Speeches: Tips on How to Write and Deliver Speeches from 51 CEOs. Brent Filson. New York: John Wiley & Sons, 1994.

Genderspeak—Men, Women, and the General Art of Verbal Self-Defense. New York: John Wiley & Sons, 1993.

How to Be an Effective Speaker. Christina Stuart. Lincolnwood, Ill.: NTC Business Books, 1988.

How to Present Like a Pro—Getting People to See Things Your Way. Lani Arredondo. New York: McGraw-Hill, 1991.

"I Can See You Naked." Ron Hoff. Kansas City: Andrews and McMeel, 1992.

Making Successful Presentations: A Self-Teaching Guide. Terry C. Smith. New York: John Wiley & Sons, 1984.

Persuasive Communication. Erwin P. Bettinghaus and Michael J. Cody. New York: Holt, Rinehart & Winston, Inc., 1987.

Presentations Plus: David People's Proven Techniques. D. A. Peoples. New York: John Wiley & Sons, 1992.

Public Speaking: A Cultural Perspective. Clella Iles Jaffe. New York: Wadsworth Publishing Co., 1995.

Smart Speaking: Sixty-Second Strategies for More Than 100 Speaking Problems and Fears. Laurie Schloff and Marcia Yudkin. New York: Plume, 1992.

Speaking with Confidence: A Guide for Public Speakers. Wanda Vassallo. Cincinnati, Ohio: Betterway Books, 1990.

Speechcraft: An Introduction to Public Speaking. Brent C. Oberg. Colorado Springs, Colo.: Meriwether Publishing Ltd., 1994.

Successful Presentations For Dummies. Malcolm Kushner. Foster City, Calif.: IDG Books Worldwide, Inc., 1996.

Winning When It Really Counts: Quick, Easy Strategies for Success in Any Speaking Situation. Arch Lustberg. New York: Simon & Schuster, 1988.

Magazines

Business Week (800) 635-1200

Entrepreneur—the Small Business Authority (800) 274-6229

Fortune (800) 621-8000

Inc.—the Magazine for Growing Companies (800) 234-0999 or (303) 604-1465

Sales and Marketing Management (800) 821-6897

U.S. News and World Report (800) 333-8130

On-line Services
America Online: (800) 827-6364, e-mail address: http://www.blue.aol.com/

Compuserve: (800) 848-8990, e-mail address: http://www.compuserve.com/

Prodigy: (914) 448-8000, e-mail address: http://www.prodigy.com/

Other Books in the Series

First Books for Business provide answers to your most pressing questions. In developing this series, we brought together an expert panel of top-notch businesspeople who shared their flair for success.

We know that the business world is chaotic and your time is valuable. So, we have taken the best of this panel's expertise and now present it in 50 colorful two-page chapters. Read it from cover to cover or use it as a reference guide. Either way, *First Books for Business* is your roadmap to business success.

Budgeting and Finance

To work effectively in today's marketplace, you must understand the importance of keeping projects "within budget." *Budgeting and Finance* demystifies the often confusing terms and paperwork associated with financial matters. This guide makes budgeting and finance principles easy to comprehend and will help you jump into the budget process with confidence. You'll learn how to:

- Determine your organization's budgetary needs
- Collect information to create a budget
- Interpret what budget and finance figures say about an organization
- Interact with others to develop a workable budget
- Read a financial statement

Negotiating

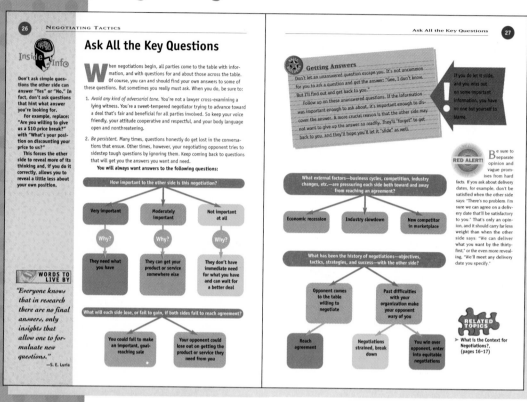

Understanding the art of negotiation is vital in your day-to-day-business dealings, whether you're negotiating a business contract with a supplier or a labor agreement with an employee. *Negotiating* teaches you how to negotiate strongly and effectively. This user-friendly guide will help you get exactly what you want, without your having to give up too much. You'll learn how to:

- Determine what you "want" versus what you "need"
- Structure the negotiations so both sides "win"
- Work with the personal dynamics of negotiating
- Get the most out of what you have to offer
- Turn around a losing trend

Sales and Marketing

Effective sales and marketing is key to the success of any business. *Sales and Marketing* sets forth the fundamental tools you need to effectively position your business. This user-friendly guide will show you how to create a marketing budget, perform research, and conduct marketing based on your organization's specific needs. You'll learn how to:

- Determine your marketing goals and objectives
- Identify and plan the strategy for reaching your markets
- Execute a tailormade marketing campaign
- Evaluate the overall success of your efforts

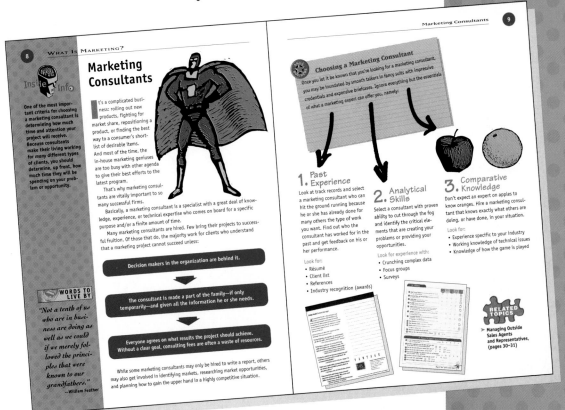

Supervising and Managing People

Whether you supervise one or many, effective management will boost your confidence and help you make your organization more productive. *Supervising and Managing People* offers smart, commonsense guidance for motivating and guiding your employees through both the short and long term. This handbook clarifies the many issues that can arise between a supervisor and employees—from creating a mentor system to creative problem solving. You'll learn how to:

- Interview and hire the best individual for each job
- Work with employees to enhance goodwill and increase productivity
- Understand the many legal issues of management in the workplace
- Deal with issues such as verbal abuse and sexual harassment
- Motivate and guide employees to reach their maximum potential

Index

Credits

Illustration

Art Parts: 6, 10, 11, 12–13, 18, 19, 20, 24, 25, 28, 29, 36, 38, 39, 48 top, 50 center, 50 bottom, 51, 54, 65, 57, 58, 59, 60, 61, 62, 63, 65, 66 bottom, 67, 76, 77, 78, 79, 89, 96, 97, 99; Frank Loose Design: 26–27, 42 top, 53, 68 top, 82–83, 84, 92, 94, 95; Image Club Graphics, Inc.: 16, 32, 70, 71, 78, 87, 88

Photography

Digital Wisdom, Inc.: 2, 40, 41, 44, 64, 66 top, 86; Image Club Graphics, Inc.: 42 center, 46, 47, 82; PhotoDisc, Inc.: 4 top, 4 center, 5, 8, 14, 15, 30, 31, 42 left, 42 right, 43, 45, 48, 49, 50 top, 68 bottom, 69, 72, 73, 75, 80, 90, 91, 92, 93, 96 top, 98, 100, 101; Pio Partners, Inc.: 4 bottom, 74